Praying with the Desert Mothers

PRAYING WITH THE DESERT MOTHERS

Mary Forman, O.S.B.

LITURGICAL PRESS
Collegeville, Minnesota

www.litpress.org

Cover design by Joachim Rhoades, o.s.b.

2	3	4	5	6	7	8

Library of Congress Cataloging-in-Publication Data

Forman, Mary, 1947–
    Praying with the Desert Mothers / Mary Forman.
        p.   cm.
    Summary: "Introduces the reader to the lives, sayings, and stories of the fourth- and fifth-century women who were foundational members of the early Christian community in the Mediterranean region; invites readers to explore their own spiritual journeys"—Provided by publisher.
    Includes bibliographical references.
    ISBN-13: 978-0-8146-1522-5 (pbk. : alk. paper)
    ISBN-10: 0-8146-1522-8 (pbk. : alk. paper)
    1. Monastic and religious life of women—History—Early church, ca. 30–600—Meditations.   2. Catholic Church—Prayer-books and devotions—English.   I. Title.

BR195.M65F67   2005
271.9'0009'015—dc22
                                                                2004031016

Contents

Preface

This book grew out of a course on the "Desert *Ammas:* Midwives of Wisdom," taught at the School of Theology, Saint John's University, Collegeville, Minnesota, beginning the summer of 1994, and was the name of a retreat. Friends and colleagues urged me to write a way of praying with these fourth and fifth-century founders of some of the first communities for women, so that their wisdom would be available to a wider audience.

Each chapter will recommend that the reader begin with a biblical passage and opening prayer, followed by stories and commentary on one or another desert mother (with an occasional story from a desert father). Finally, a reflection exercise will be offered as an invitation to discover and to experience the reality of the wisdom of these early sources. In this way, one is encouraged to pray with the desert mothers and come to know their wisdom in one's own life. At the end of the book a bibliography for further reading is provided.

I wish to thank the sisters of my Benedictine community, the Monastery of Saint Gertrude, Cottonwood, Idaho, for their loving support of this work. Friends and colleagues have been invaluable in their contributions to my studies over the years. Special thanks to students in the "Desert *Ammas*" course who, over the years, provided valuable insights and questions.

Some material first appeared in an essay, entitled "Desert *Ammas:* Midwives of Wisdom" in *Nova Doctrina Vetusque: Essays on Early Christianity in Honor of Fredric W. Schlatter, S.J.*, ed. Douglas Kries and Catherine Brown Tkacz (New York: Peter Lang,

1999) 187–201; and "Amma Syncletica: A Spirituality of Experience," *Vox Benedictina* 10.2 (Winter 1993) 199–237. I wish to thank Justin Pelegano at Peter Lang and Margot King at Peregrina Publishing Company, for granting permission to use these articles. In addition, E. Rozanne Elder, Director, Cistercian Publications, and Barbara McCormick, Permissions Department, Paulist Press, graciously granted permission to use excerpts from their publications in this book.

I dedicate this book to all the *ammas* in my own life.

Introduction to the Desert Mothers

OPENING REFLECTION: Sirach 24:1-3, 12-19

O God Most High, you have made each of us like one of the trees of the East, by planting the root of your love deep within each of our calls to follow you. May we give back to you by the fruits of our lives, a portion of your great love and wisdom that you have bestowed on us. May your own presence, so gracious and generous, fill us with whatever graces you desire for us this day. We ask this in the name of Wisdom Incarnate, Jesus Christ our Lord. Amen.

INTRODUCTORY REMARKS

The women who came to be known as mothers of the early ascetical-monastic tradition represent the rich diversity of cultural backgrounds and regions in which they are found. Early twentieth-century scholarship on the origins of monasticism in the fourth and fifth centuries tended to hold a monolithic view of the movement of the monastic impulse beginning in the East—particularly Egypt, and making its way via translations of the *Life of Antony* and the stories of the heroes of the Egyptian desert—and ending in the West, in Italy and southern Gaul. This approach all but ignored the contributions of the female leaders of households of Christian women in the West who made pilgrimage to the East, supported whole colonies of male monastic communities in Egypt, Palestine, and surrounding areas, and established monasteries both for men and women. Recent translations of the lives and stories of these

1

women, frequently referred to in the literature as *ammas*, have brought to light the unique role in history these women played in the actual foundations of monasticism.

Amma is the term designated for a "spiritual mother," an equivalent term to *abba*, the term for "spiritual father." *Amma* refers to the *ability* one had to become a spiritual guide for another and is not explicitly associated with the role of abbess or superior.[1]

STORIES AND COMMENTARY

An understanding of *amma* as spiritual guide can be gained from reading a delightful tale told of the monk Zossima and his encounter with Mary of Egypt, a reformed prostitute, who lived as a wandering *amma* in the desert. The story opens with Zossima living a pious and blameless monastic life in the monastery in Palestine where he had been since he was a weaned child. In his mid-life (at age fifty-three) he began to be tormented by a temptation to think he had attained perfection in everything and needed no further teaching. Once, while he was wondering if there were any other monk who exceeded him in virtue, an angel appeared to him, who informed him that he had "done as well as any man could" in the monastic life, but that more was in store for him. He was bidden to leave his native land, like Abraham, and to "go to the monastery which lies near the river Jordan."[2]

So Zossima left his home monastery and followed the Jordan River until he found the monastery to which the angel directed him. The abbot of the place extended him the usual greetings of hospitality of prostration and prayer and then asked Zossima

---

[1] Irénée Hausherr, *Spiritual Direction in the Early Christian East*, Cistercian Studies 116, trans. Anthony P. Gythiel (Kalamazoo: Cistercian Publications, 1990) 277.

[2] Benedicta Ward, "St. Mary of Egypt: The Liturgical Icon of Repentance," *Harlots of the Desert: A Study in Repentance in Early Monastic Sources* (London & Oxford: Mowbray, 1987) ch. 2, 37–38.

from where and why he had come to such a humble place. Zossima responded that the *where* was not important, but the reason was in order to make spiritual progress; besides, he had heard that the abbot was one who "could draw a soul to intimate familiarity with Christ." The abbot replied that God alone was healer of human infirmity, but that if Zossima were moved by the love of God, he was welcome to stay and be fed by the grace of the Spirit of the Good Shepherd.[3]

Zossima stayed in that monastery and became very edified by the fervor of life he found there. On the first Sunday of Lent, all the monks met in the church to pray for each other, to receive a blessing, and then went beyond the gates of the monastery out into the desert with a few provisions to fast and pray. The rule they solemnly kept was to enter into solitude and not to know how the others lived and fasted during Lent. On the twentieth day of his walking in solitude, Zossima came across what he first thought was an apparition; on coming closer he found it was "a woman and she was naked, her body black as if scorched by the fierce heat of the sun, the hair on her head was white as wool and short, coming down only to the neck."[4]

> [Zossima] knelt down and asked her to give him the customary blessing. She also knelt down. So they both remained on the ground asking one another for a blessing. After a long time the woman said to Zossima, "*Father* Zossima, it is proper for you to give the blessing and say the prayer, for you have the dignity of the office of a priest, and for many years you have stood at the holy table and offered the sacrifice of Christ." These words threw Zossima into greater dread, he trembled and was covered with a sweat of death. But at last, breathing with difficulty, he said to her, "O *Mother* in the spirit, it is plain from this insight that all your life you have dwelt with God and have nearly died to the world. It is plain above all that grace is given you since you called me by my name and recognized me as a priest although you have never seen

---

[3] Ibid., "St. Mary of Egypt," ch. 3, 38.
[4] Ibid., ch. 7, 41.

> me before. But since grace is recognized not by office but by gifts
> of the Spirit, bless me, for God's sake, and pray for me out of the
> kindness of your heart." So the woman gave way to the wish of the
> old man, and said, "Blessed is God who cares for the salvation of
> souls." Zossima answered "Amen," and they both rose from their
> knees.[5]

The woman was puzzled as to why Zossima had come to her,
thinking that the Holy Spirit has sent him to perform a service for
her in due time. She inquired about the Christian leadership in
the empire and how the church was fairing. He responded:

> "By your holy prayers, *mother*, Christ has given lasting peace every-
> where. But hear the request of an unworthy monk and pray to the
> Lord for the whole world and for me, a sinner, that my wander-
> ing through the desert should not be without fruit." She answered
> him, "It is only right, *Father* Zossima, that you who have the office
> of a priest should pray for me and for all; but we must be obedi-
> ent so I shall willingly do what you bid me." With these words, she
> turned to the East and raising her eyes to heaven and stretching
> up her hands she began to pray moving her lips in silence, so that
> almost nothing intelligible could be heard. So Zossima could not
> understand anything of her prayer.[6]

As she continued in prayer, even to the point of levitation, he
became quite terrified and cried out within himself, "Lord, have
mercy!"

Twice in this account Zossima the priest "father" calls Mary
"mother," that is, *amma*, because she is a "Mother in the spirit."
Of significance in the story is the fact that the normal cultural
expectation that a Christian woman seek a blessing of a priest is
reversed (it is worth noting that this story comes to us from the
fifth century). Instead Zossima the "father" asks a blessing of the
"mother." When later he petitions her to pray for him, she is at
first reluctant: "It is only right, Father Zossima, that you who have

---

[5] Ibid., chs. 9–10, 42. Italics indicate my emphasis.
[6] Ibid., chs. 9–10, 42–43. Italics indicate my emphasis.

the office of a priest should pray for me and for [us] all." Her hesitation to extend a blessing, the cultural prerogative of the priest, is transformed into awareness of their mutuality in Christ, and she responds: "but *we* must be obedient so I shall willingly do what you bid me."

That blessing comes straight from the Spirit dwelling in her heart, so she can speak it. Her blessing is a blessing that God desires for all people. Her blessing has always struck me. It is so exquisitely short, but contains the kernel of God's desire for us: "Blessed is God who cares for the salvation of souls."

In the rest of the narrative, Mary ministered to Zossima by telling the story of her past sin and call to repentance. As a consequence of her confession, a friendship of hearts developed between them. In the process, Zossima learned about one who exceeded him in virtue because she allowed the grace of the Holy Spirit to work salvation in her.

This capacity to cooperate with the grace of the Spirit, making of woman a channel of that grace to others, is the reason Mary and other women of spiritual strength were called *ammas*. Three women—Sarah, Theodora, and Syncletica—are specifically designated *ammas* and their apophthegms, or wise sayings, are found in the alphabetical collection of *The Sayings of the Desert Fathers*.[7] The very fact that their sayings appear in the collection indicates that their teaching had "doctrinal value." This means that the compilers of the sayings did not discriminate on the basis of gender in their selection of sayings. Even further, these women exercised a spiritual maternity on a par with the spiritual paternity of the *abbas;* thus they could transmit spiritual doctrine with the same right as monks. The only thing they could not do was absolve sins sacramentally.[8] We encounter the distinction between

---

[7] *The Sayings of the Desert Fathers: The Alphabetical Collection*, Cistercian Studies 59, trans. Benedicta Ward (London & Oxford: Mowbray/U.S.A.: Cistercian Publications, 1975) Theodora, 82–84; Sarah, 229–30; Syncletica, 230–35.

[8] Josep M. Soler, "Les Mères du désert et la maternité spirituelle," *Collectanea Cisterciensia* 48 (1986) 239.

teaching of spiritual matters and the priestly functions of preaching in the story of St. Pachomius' sister Mary, *amma* and superior of the women's community in the Thebaid, Upper Egypt:

> Pachomius' sister, whose name was Mary and who had been a virgin from childhood, heard about him and she came north to see him at Tabennesi. When he was told she had arrived, he sent the brother who watched at the door of the monastery to tell her, "I see you have learned I am alive. Do not be distressed, however, because you have not seen me. But if you wish to share in this holy life so that you may find mercy before God, examine yourself on every point. The brothers will build a place for you to retire to. And doubtless, for your sake the Lord will call others to you, and they will be saved because of you. Man has no other hope in this world but to do good before he departs from the body and is led to the place where he shall be judged and rewarded according to his works." When she heard these words from the lips of the porter she wept, and she accepted the advice. When our *father* Pachomius had found that her heart inclined to the good and right life, he immediately sent the brothers over to build a monastery for her in that village, a short distance from his own monastery; it included a small oratory.[9]

In keeping with the gospel directive to forsake family for the sake of Christ, Pachomius makes no effort physically to greet his blood sister Mary. This practice is in keeping with a concern to avoid the enmeshed family relationships that were part of the Egyptian culture. However, sensing that her purpose might be to follow Christ in the monastic way of life, he provides the means to foster that vocation by having the brothers build her a monastery not far from his own. The story about Mary in "The Bohairic Life of Pachomius," chapter 27, further relates:

[9] "The Bohairic Life of Pachomius," ch. 27: 'Pachomius sister founds a monastery for women,' in *Pachomian Koinonia I: The Life of Saint Pachomius*, Cistercian Studies 45, trans. Armand Veilleux (Kalamazoo: Cistercian Publications, 1980) 49–51. My italics are for emphasis.

Later on many heard about her and came to live with her. They practised *ascesis* eagerly with her, and she was their *mother* and their worthy *elder* until her death.

When our *father* Pachomius saw that the number of [these women] was increasing somewhat, he appointed an old man called Apa Peter, whose "speech was seasoned with salt" to be their *father* and to preach frequently to them on the Scriptures for their souls' salvation. [Pachomius] also wrote down in a book the rules of the brothers and sent them to them through [Peter], so that they might learn them.

If ever any of the brothers who had not yet attained perfection wanted to visit one of his relatives among [the sisters], [Pachomius] sent him through his house-master's direction to the holy old man Apa Peter who in turn sent word to their *mother* to come out with her and another sister. They sat down together with great propriety until the visit came to an end; then they got up, prayed and withdrew.

When one of [the sisters] died, they brought her to the oratory and first their *mother* covered her with a shroud. Then the old man Apa Peter sent word to our *father* Pachomius who chose experienced brothers and sent them to the monastery with [Apa Peter]. They proceeded to the assembly room and stood in the entry-way chanting psalms with gravity until [the deceased] was prepared for burial. Then she was placed on a bier and carried to the mountain. The virgin sisters followed behind the bier while their *father* walked after them and their *mother* before them. When the deceased was buried, they prayed for her and returned with great sorrow to their dwelling.[10]

This story reveals several practices that would find their way down through the ages of monastic life for women. The superior is called *mother*, not because of any physical nurturing nor to transfer a familial image, but because she is a "worthy elder," that is,

[10] "The Bohairic Life of Pachomius," ch. 27, in *Pachomian Koinonia I: The Life of Saint Pachomius*, 49–51. Italics indicate my emphasis.

one able to impart wisdom to the sisters of her community. She herself would be thought to be an exemplar of *ascesis,* that is the observances of a way of life that leads to holiness and salvation.

Moreover, in the story there is an *abba,* or wise male elder, whose responsibility it is to preach the Scriptures in such a way that his "speech was seasoned with salt." This expression does not refer to the "salty" speech of sailors! Rather, an abba's preaching style was to be such that the words conveyed the essence or spice, if you will, of God's spirit and "preserved" the salvation of its hearers.

Those sisters who entered a religious community before Vatican II remember the propriety of going two-by-two together, as noted in the story. In the early days, male relatives were not to see their sisters, mothers, cousins, aunts, or nieces without chaperones being present. In an ancient culture that carefully guarded women's reputations from gossip and rumors, such chaperonage was to be expected. But more than reputation is at stake; the conversation itself was enclosed in prayer, so that the God of their mutual vocation would be the center of the visit.

The death of one of the sisters was cause for visitation of another sort. Brothers, advanced in the monastic life, were sent to attend the services of the deceased sister. While the women prepared her body for burial, the brothers chanted psalms. For the funeral procession, most likely the bier with the sister's body was carried on the shoulders of the monks for the climb up the mountain to the cemetery. Amma Mary came next, followed by the community, and then their chaplain, Apa Peter. The sister was buried with the customary prayers for the dead, commendation of the body into God's care, and, of course, expressions of sorrow, so appropriate at a time of grief.

Unfortunately, little else is known of Amma Mary and her community other than what this brief glimpse recorded in the *Life of Pachomius* reveals. There are no records from the hand of a sister-chronicler of the community to tell us more about these women and their monastic way of life. One can surmise that their superior was revered as "the mother of virgins," as Pachomius' biographer remembers her. She herself covers the body of her deceased sister with the shroud. We can imagine her clothing the body of Christ and preparing it for burial, much like Mary of Magdala, who wished to anoint Jesus' body housed in the tomb after his death. No doubt Amma Mary had also sat in vigil with the sister while she lay dying.

CONTEMPORARY EXAMPLE

I too remember once sitting with Sister Felicity, early infirmarian of my own monastery, as she lay dying. One of her Swiss countrywomen, Sister Gonzaga, was keeping vigil the hour before. When I told Sister Gonzaga that she was free to go, she looked at me and said, "Sister Mary, I would like to stay awhile longer. I've often wondered if I had lived at the time of Jesus, what kind of disciple would I have been and, when he was dying, where I would have been. But now Jesus has given me this opportunity as I am waiting with him as Sister Felicity is waiting to go home to God. God has answered my desire. So stay with me and we will pray together." And we did.

Sister Gonzaga taught me, as Amma Mary taught her own sisters, how to wait in silence and prayer with the dying Christ until the soul of the beloved one would be called home to its Maker. Sister Gonzaga witnessed to me the deep faith of our monastic foremothers who knew how to be present, tender, and watchful.

REFLECTION EXERCISES

You are welcome to enter into one or the other reflection exercises as you feel called. For the first, choose a time when you kept vigil with a friend or family member who was ill or dying. You may wish to ask the Lord to bring the memory of that occasion to your awareness. Looking back, how did you respond to this call to spend one hour with Christ in prayer? Invite the

Lord to reveal to you what you were learning at the time. What wisdom lives in your heart because of this sacred waiting time? What do you desire to tell the Lord who visited you with the grace of this experience?

A second possible meditation is on the gift of friendship, which called forth the blessing of a deepening relationship with God, that is, a time when you knew in your experience that this other person, in whom Christ visited you, would bring forth gifts in you, which you did not at that time know were latent within you. Let the Lord bring the memory back of the gift of that friendship—say a significant conversation exchanged between you and this friend, and the ways in which you were changed by the encounter. I invite you to savor the memory and then ask the Spirit of Wisdom to share with you the fruit of that gift that has been borne in your life since that day. Then what return would you like to make for what the Lord has bestowed on you?

FURTHER SCRIPTURAL PASSAGES FOR PRAYER

Tobit 1:16-18, 2:1-8	Tobit buries the dead

Mark 16:1-8/
  Luke 24:1-12
	Mary Magdalene and other women come
	  to anoint Jesus' body

John 20:1-18	Mary's encounter with the Risen Lord
Ruth 1:1-18	The friendship between Naomi and Ruth
John 15:1-17	The vine and branches and friendship with the Lord
Romans 12:9-21	Life in community

1

Ammas as Midwives of Wisdom

OPENING REFLECTION: Wisdom 9:9-12

Lord of all wisdom, Solomon prayed for the gift of your wisdom and his prayer was answered. Today, we too pray for wisdom as we honor your loving presence within and among us. May our hearts be made suitable dwelling places of your abiding Triune presence, so that we may be a gift of blessing to others and be guided discreetly in all things this day. We pray, in the name of the Father, and of the Son, and of the Holy Spirit. Amen.

INTRODUCTORY REMARKS

This chapter addresses the desert mothers as midwives of wisdom. The expression "midwives" conveys the notion that the *ammas* were *pneumataphores*, or bearers of the spirit.[1] In other words, they were women capable of listening to the hearts of those around them in such a way that the Spirit birthed Christ in

---

[1] Irénée Hausherr, *Spiritual Direction in the Early Christian East*, Cistercian Studies 116, trans. Anthony P. Gythiel (Kalamazoo: Cistercian Publications, 1990) 341, gives the following definition in his glossary: *"Pneumataphore*, a bearer *(pherein)* of the Spirit *(pneuma)*, a synonym of *pneumatikos*, 'one who is spiritual.' Refers to the person who bears the Spirit or is borne by the Spirit, depending on tonic accent. Hence, inspired, prophetic. [Bilaniuk, P. B., 'The Monk as Pneumataphor in the Writings of Basil the Great,' in *Diakonia* 15 (1980) 49–63]." Because *ammas* are "spiritual mothers" (Hausherr, 26 and 277), they are no less *pneumataphores* than their male counterparts, the "spiritual fathers."

their hearts and in their lives; and so they stood as midwives to that unfolding experience of an ever fuller dimension of Christ living in the hearts of the women and the men whom they served and to whom they listened. The *ammas* had a profound sense of what it means to allow another to know the salvation of God. That was a deeply important awareness for them. As they themselves had experienced God's salvation—their being healed, their being saved, their being brought into the profound love of God—they could not help but desire salvation for the men and women around them. Some of the ways that they helped to birth that experience was in the art of spiritual direction. In whatever way they heard themselves called by God to share the wealth of their giftedness, they readily gave. In some cases their physical wealth made possible the establishment of places of prayer and of monasteries where people could come to experience God. In many other ways they shared their gifts so that the birth of Christ would occur evermore fully in the lives of others. In terms of spiritual direction, sometimes that was a very indirect kind of an experience, or it might be the treatment of an ailment from which someone was suffering.

STORIES AND COMMENTARY

One such example is a story told by Palladius, a pilgrim who traveled around Egypt and Palestine collecting the stories of famous *abbas* and *ammas* and then wrote those down so that others would know about them. One of the people with whom he was enamored—and he knew the whole family—was Melania the Elder. He records the story of how Evagrius, a young man who had been involved in a love affair with a government official's wife, had to leave Cappadocia because, if he had been caught, his crime would have been punishable as a capital offense. So he fled Cappadocia. Evagrius had known Basil of Caesarea who had ordained him lector, and he was ordained a deacon by Gregory of Nazianzen, Basil's close friend. Evagrius boarded a boat and traveled across the Mediterranean to the Holy Land, and there met up with Melania the Elder, who had established a monastery on the Mount of Olives.

When the Roman lady, Melania, greeted him, he said nothing about his past life and his indiscretion. While he was staying at her monastery, he developed a fever that lasted six months. Of course, she was concerned for him, so she sent in physicians to heal him but they could not find the source of the problem. He started wasting away at which point Melania went into him and said: "'Son, I am not pleased with your long sickness. Tell me what is in your mind, for your sickness is not beyond God's aid.' Then he confessed the whole story. She told him: 'Promise me by the Lord that you mean to aim at the monastic life, and even though I am a sinner, I will pray that you be given a lease on life.' He agreed, and was well again in a matter of days. He got up, received a change of clothing at her hands, then left and took himself to the mountain of Nitria in Egypt."[2]

And he stayed in that region the rest of his life. Now Melania detected with her spiritual sight what the doctors were unable to find, namely, that Evagrius had made a promise to God to become a monk and had reneged on that promise once he had left Cappadocia. Moreover, she trusted in the God of her prayer, mindful that she herself was a sinner. Her *surety* contrasted with Evagrius' *uncertainty*. Her detection of the source of the illness and her prayer brought about the healing of this young man, who would eventually become the first systematician of the monastic life and whose writings would exert a profound influence on Cassian, one of Benedict's predecessors. One wonders how the course of Western monasticism would have unfolded had this child of Melania's prayer not met up with Melania. While the midwife has often been neglected by church historians, the son of her intercessory prayer has been remembered for centuries.

[2]"Evagrius #7–9," in *Palladius: The Lausiac History*, Ancient Christian Writers 34, trans. Robert T. Meyer (Westminster, Md.: The Newman Press/London: Longmans, Green and Co., 1965) 112–13. www.paulistpress.com.

This midwife of his spirit sent him back to his original call to live faithfully to the God who saved him. Moreover, she clothed him in the monastic habit.

She undertook to be responsible with respect to Evagrius' salvation, as well as his physical well-being. Her care for Evagrius represents the ancient practice of being *custos animi*, that is, custody of the heart/soul. This implies three different elements: "1) responsibility for another person's well-being and ultimate salvation, 2) a knowledge of his or her inner life, [and] 3) a spiritual dimension"[3] to the relationship. Her listening intently to Evagrius' vision, revelatory of his inner chaos, became the medicine he needed to become well. Other accounts of her reveal her profound knowledge of the Scriptures,[4] from which she drew spiritual nourishment, not only for herself, but also for others.

Moreover, she was a formidable advocate of Christian asceticism. One could not meet Melania and not have the course of one's life changed. She was able to persuade her nephew-in-law, Apronianus, and his wife, Avita, to embrace the life.[5] Later on, her granddaughter, Melania the Younger, along with her husband, Pinian, would settle in Thagaste, first home of Augustine, where they financed many charitable and monastic projects from their vast wealth.[6] They used that wealth to establish monasteries all

[3] Brian Patrick McGuire, *Friendship and Community: The Monastic Experience 350–1250*, Cistercian Studies 95 (Kalamazoo: Cistercian Publications, 1988) xvi.

[4] According to Palladius, *The Lausiac History*, "Silvania #3," pp. 136–37: "[Melania] was most erudite and fond of literature . . . going through every writing of the ancient commentators—three million lines of Origen and two and a half million lines of Gregory, Stephen, Pierius, Basil, and other worthy men . . . dredging through each work seven or eight times." www.paulistpress.com.

[5] See "More About Melania the Elder," 54.4, in *Palladius: The Lausiac History*, 135; www.paulistpress.com. This English translation by Meyer indicates that Palladius calls "Abita" a cousin to Melania, whereas the edition by Cuthbert Butler (p. 147) calls her "niece." In his stemma for Melania's family tree, Francis X. Murphy indicates that Avita was the daughter of Melania's sister Antonia; see his "Melania the Elder: A Biographical Note," *Traditio* 5 (1947) 63.

[6] See *Palladius: Lausiac History* 54.4 (www.paulistpress.com) for Melania the Elder's influence on her granddaughter. See the following concerning Melania the Younger and Pinian settling at Thagaste: Augustine's "Epistula CXXIV," Corpus

along the Mediterranean. Another distant relative of the older Melania, Paulinus of Nola, and his wife, Therasia, embraced the ascetical life and established a site of pilgrimage, a hostel and monastery at Nola (near Naples) in honor of St. Felix.[7] From this one matriarch of living faith sprang a whole legacy of spiritual children who were dedicated to the pursuit of holiness.

A different example of midwifery can be seen in a story told by Amma Theodora.

> "7. Amma Theodora also said, 'There was a monk, who, because of the great number of temptations said, "I will go away from here." As he was putting on his sandals, he saw another man who was also putting on his sandals and this other monk said to him, "Is it on my account that you are going away? Because I go before you wherever you are going."'"[8]

The scene was likely a conversation between Amma Theodora and a monk, who was struggling with the temptation to leave his vocation or desirous to go somewhere else where temptations were less severe. Theodora did not give direct advice nor does she say

---

Scriptorum Ecclesiasticorum Latinorum 44, Pars III: Ep. 124–84, 1–2, ed. Al. Goldbacher (Vienna: F. Tempsky/Leipzig: G. Freitag, 1904); and Gerontius, *The Life of Melania the Younger*, Studies in Women and Religion 14, trans. Elizabeth A. Clark (Lewiston, N.Y.: Mellen, 1984) chs. 21–22, p. 44.

[7] Joseph T. Lienhard, *Paulinus of Nola and Early Western Monasticism*. With a Study of the Chronology of His Works and Annotated Bibliography, 1879–1976, Theophaneia Beitrage zur Religions- und Kirchengeschichte des Altertums 28 (Cologne–Bonn: Peter Hanstein Verlag GMBH, 1977) 68, 70–72, documents the establishment of this monastery-shrine under the patronage of the martyr Felix. References to details of the patron's life are recorded by Paulinus in his *Carmina* 15, 16, 18, 21, 23, 24, and 26–29. Paulinus is one of our sources for information concerning Melania the Elder, in his letter 29.5–14. In ch. 12 of this letter, he tells of her visit to Nola, where she was welcomed by her children and grandchildren. The English trans. can be found in *Letters of St. Paulinus of Nola*, vol. 2, Ancient Christian Writers 36, trans. P. G. Walsh (Westminster, Md.: The Newman Press/London: Longmans, Green & Co., 1967) Ep. 29.5–14: pp. 105–18; ch. 12: pp. 114–15. www.paulistpress.com.

[8] "Theodora #7," in *The Sayings of the Desert Fathers: The Alphabetical Collection*, Cistercian Studies 59, trans. Benedicta Ward (London & Oxford: Mowbray/U.S.A.: Cistercian Publications, 1975) 84.

who the second monk was in her story. Rather, like a good teacher, she posed a kind of parable or story in which the monk was to see himself and then "draw the inescapable conclusion: we each take ourselves wherever we go."[9] Her method of spiritual direction was a form of "indirection" under which lies three assumptions, according to the contemporary scholar Roberta Bondi: "The restless monk who undoubtedly [1] could not hear direct advice about running away [2] could hear the story and draw the conclusion, and [3] he was able to hear it because the amma did not stand between him and what she was trying to get him to see."[10]

The capacity to distinguish spirits lying behind behaviors was another of the valuable gifts of midwives of the spirit. Amma Syncletica, a fifth-century spiritual elder, said: "There is a grief that is useful, and there is a grief that is destructive. The first sort consists in weeping over one's own faults and weeping over the weakness of one's neighbours, in order not to destroy one's purpose, and attach oneself to the perfect good. But there is also a grief that comes from the enemy, full of mockery, which some call *accidie*. This spirit must be cast out, mainly by prayer and psalmody."[11]

A sadness that is beneficial has a far different quality to it than one that leads to depression, guilt, or the subtle temptation of *acedia*—that state of mind which, because it is so reliant on self-effort, encourages giving up the pursuit of holiness altogether. In distinguishing the two kinds of grief, Syncletica reflects the teaching of Evagrius and Cassian.[12] Her unique addition to Cassian's

---

[9] Roberta C. Bondi, "The Abba and Amma in Early Monasticism: The First Pastoral Counselors?" *Journal of Pastoral Care* 40:4 (December 1986) 320.

[10] Ibid., 320.

[11] "Syncletica # 27," in *The Sayings of the Desert Fathers: The Alphabetical Collection*, Cistercian Studies 59, trans. Benedicta Ward (London & Oxford: Mowbray/U.S.A.: Cistercian Publications, 1975) 235.

[12] Cassian, "Inst. 9.1," in Jean Cassien, *Institutions Cénobitiques*, Sources chrétiennes [SC] 109, ed. Jean-Claude Guy (Paris: Les Éditions du Cerf, 1965) 370; "Inst. 10.1," SC 109.384: "There is a sixth contest for us that the Greeks call *acedia*, which we can name weariness or anxiety of heart. This is related to sadness, as is better known by experience to solitaries and is a frequent and more hostile enemy to those dwelling in the desert"; "Inst. 9.9–10," SC 109.376, distinguishes

teaching is the notion of the beneficial grief of weeping over one's neighbors. Not only does Syncletica discern the difference between the spirits behind grief, she is able to recommend the remedies of prayer and psalmody. The kind of dejection that leads to abandonment of the monastic vocation is one that tempts the monastic to give up prayer and psalmody. Thus the very practices one is tempted to cast aside provide the means of healing.

In our final example of spiritual midwifery, Amma Theodora gives an explanation of how one recognizes a true spiritual guide. "The same amma said that a teacher ought to be a stranger to the desire for domination, vain-glory, and pride; one should not be able to fool him by flattery, nor blind him by gifts, nor conquer him by the stomach, nor dominate him by anger; but he should be patient, gentle and humble as far as possible; he must be tested and without partisanship, full of concern, and a lover of souls."[13]

Theodora teaches that the virtues of true midwives of people's spiritual lives are patience, gentleness, and humility—the complete opposites to domination, vainglory, and pride. The qualities[14] of such a discerning pneumataphore are tests that have determined the fruit; a lack of partisanship, that is, freedom from an ardent or militant support of a cause, person, party, or idea; and being a lover of souls. It is noteworthy that Theodora recommends all these qualities together. In other words, it is not enough to love people in order to be a good spiritual director. One must also be discerning, that is, subject to the testings of the spirit, and reveal a certain detachment from any sole part of things. Attachment to the part takes away from the whole, that is, God's deepest desire for that person.

---

a dejection or sadness producing despair of salvation from one, which leads to penitence for sin.

   [13]"Theodora #5," in *The Sayings of the Desert Fathers*, 83–84.

   [14] For a fuller elaboration of these qualities, refer to the article by Josep M. Soler, "Les Mères du désert et la maternité spirituelle," *Collectanea Cisterciensia* 48 (1986) 245–47.

CONTEMPORARY EXAMPLE

Many women and men today are hungering in their spiritual lives for someone to walk with them, to listen to them in ways that make possible their believing in God's love for them. Probably one of the greatest needs in our church today is for depth listening to others' experiences that empowers them to be fully the gift that they are. I recall when I worked in a rural parish, a young Hispanic woman came to me asking if it were possible to have experiences of God. When I said, "Yes, I believe it is possible," she began to relate several contemplative, even mystical, moments of her prayer life. But when she had tried to share them with the parish priest, he had told her that he did not believe in mysticism, nor did he expect that anyone her age could be having such experiences. Thank God she was courageous enough to keep on looking for someone who could accompany her in her journey in faith and prayer, and so be validated as the woman of deep prayer God had gifted her to be. Of course, the spiritual life is not solely about religious experiences. The deepest sign of God's indwelling is how one treats the neighbor. This woman was renowned for her care of those poorer than herself.

REFLECTION EXERCISES

I invite you to spend some moments in prayer pondering the men and women who have accompanied you in your search for God. You may recall a significant retreat leader, an elder in the community, a spiritual friend, or mentor, who listened carefully to your journey, perhaps challenged you, and also prayed with you to make a wise choice or decision in your life. As you reflect upon that person's contribution in your life, pause to recall the gifts that were made available to you in that relationship. You may wish to ask the Lord how the Divine One has seen the consequences of that choice/decision. Then at the end of your reflection, I invite you to write a prayer of thanksgiving for the blessing of that *amma/abba* in your life.

If you wish, you may also want to reflect on a time in which you served in the role of mentor, *amma,* guide, or spiritual friend with another. You may wish to consider what circumstances brought about your coming together. What gifts of presence did the other call forth from you? How were you enriched by his/her need for listening, prayerful support, love, mercy, etc.? What did you discover about yourself from this exchange of gifts? Then, at the end of your reflection, I invite you to write a prayer of thanksgiving for the blessing of being called to serve as listener/guide in the other's life.

FURTHER SCRIPTURAL PASSAGES FOR PRAYER

Proverbs 8:22-31	In praise of Lady Wisdom
Psalm 8	Divine Majesty and human dignity
John 16:12-15	The Spirit's guidance into all truth
Romans 5:1-11	Faith, hope and love in Christ's salvation

2

Ammas as Scripture Scholars

OPENING REFLECTION: Wisdom 7:22-27

O Wisdom, whom we seek, be with us and unfold to us that particular manifestation of your spirit you most desire us to receive this day. May we savor the bestowal of your blessedness in our lives, so in turn we may be a source of blessing to whomever you send us. We desire the gift of being friends of God, as God may design and desire in our lives. We entrust ourselves into the tender care of your benevolence, as we pray in your holy name. Amen.

INTRODUCTORY REMARKS

"Wisdom" was the gift that allowed the *ammas* to distinguish one spirit from another. Discernment, the most important of all virtues, is intimately linked with wisdom, at least in the Latin verb. *Sapere,* which initially meant "to taste" and "to have good taste," eventually came to mean, "to be discriminating," "to discern," and "to be wise."[1]

Apart from the etymology of words, "holy wisdom," or *Hagia Sophia* as she came to be known in the Wisdom books of the Septuagint, refers to the divine Word and Wisdom, who "was

---

[1] See Mary Forman, *"Sapere*—Tasting the Wisdom of the Monastic Tradition: The Biblical and Patristic Roots of Discerning," *Benedictines* XLIX:1 (Summer 1996) 33.

associated with creation—either as the master craftsman at God's side, fashioning all things well, or as the wide-eyed child who took delight in God's inhabited earth" (Prov 8:30).[2] In the book of Wisdom 7:22-27, the passage for the opening prayer, Wisdom became the image of God and queen consort, the partner of God, and bestower of every good.

In the Christian Scriptures, Sophia became associated with Christ, particularly in the writings of Paul, who asserts Christ as "the power and the wisdom of God" (1 Cor 1:24). He addressed these words to some Corinthian Christians who

> had adopted a charismatic spirituality that laid great stress on "wisdom" and "gnosis," visions and revelations, eloquent preaching, ecstatic trances, speaking in tongues, and similar phenomena . . . he tried to make their religion more christocentric by proclaiming that in Christ alone they could find everything they sought through the cultivation of exotic mystical experience. Above all, Christ alone was the true Sophia, the "secret and hidden wisdom of God . . . decreed before the ages for our glorification" (1 Cor 2:7).[3]

STORIES AND COMMENTARY

The pursuit of philosophy (the Greek word *philosophia* means "love of wisdom") in early Hellenistic Christianity was strongly associated with living a deeply committed Christian life. This connection is shown in an excerpt from the *Life of Macrina* by her brother, Gregory of Nyssa, in which he related of her the following:

> Our narrative was not based on hearsay, but we talked with detailed knowledge of things our own experience has taught us, without appealing to any outside testimony; for the maiden we spoke of was no stranger to my family so that I had to learn from others the

[2] Barbara Newman, "The Pilgrimage of Christ–Sophia," *Vox Benedictina* 9:1 (Winter 1992) 11. For a study of the development of the Christ–Sophia motif, read the whole of Newman's article, pp. 9–37.

[3] Ibid., 16.

marvels of her life. No, we had the same parents and she was, so to speak, a votive offering of the fruits to come, the first offshoot of our mother's womb. And so, since you were convinced that the story of her good deeds would be of some use because you thought that a life of this quality should not be forgotten for the future and that she who had raised herself through philosophy to the highest limit of human virtue should not pass along this way veiled and in silence, I thought it good to obey you and tell her story, as briefly as I could, in a simple unaffected narrative.[4]

Thus he writes to a very good friend of his that what he is about to unfold is the philosophy of Macrina's life. One pauses on the words, "she who had raised herself through philosophy to the highest limit of human virtue should not pass this way veiled and in silence." Kevin Corrigan, translator of this work and himself a professor of philosophy, states that this *vita* and its parallel text, *On the Soul and Resurrection*—a long dialogue between Macrina and her brother Gregory—were intended to portray Macrina as a second Socrates, who searched "for a living wisdom which involved the conversion of the whole person to the Good."[5] Such is the spirit of Gregory's use of the term "philosophy." However, the food for Macrina's philosophy was not that of the rhetorical school, but the teachings of the Scriptures. Her wisdom "embraces the whole of human life: prayer, manual work, hospitality, care of the sick, of the poor and the dying. It is a life entirely given to God, a life lived 'on the boundaries' of human nature. It includes a vibrant intellectuality, life-long study and a spirit of true inquiry, and it culminates in the divine love of a *person*, Christ."[6]

In this *vita* Macrina is portrayed with all the manifestations of the desert *amma*. First of all, she lived a life hidden at Annisa by the Iris River, a life that was in some form a desert; she was far from the arenas of controversies and theological preoccupations

---

[4] Gregory, Bishop of Nyssa, *The Life of Saint Macrina*, trans. Kevin Corrigan (Toronto, Ont.: Peregrina Publishing Co., 1987) 26–27.

[5] Ibid., 63, n. 2.

[6] Corrigan, Introduction to *Saint Macrina*, 23.

of her three brother-bishops: Basil of Caesarea, Gregory of Nyssa, and Peter of Sebaste. Secondly, she was an *amma* who, even as a young teen, served as "father, teacher, guide, mother, counsellor in every good"[7] to her youngest brother Peter, the last of ten children. She never left her own mother, whom she persuaded to join in the ascetical life of their household community, where Macrina eventually became superior of the whole community, comprised of men and virgins and household servants, each living in separate dwellings.[8] She was a spiritual midwife in the sense that Gregory looked upon her as "my teacher in everything."[9] It was Macrina, who, when her brother Basil came home from rhetorical school all puffed up with his new knowledge, took him to task and won him over to the pursuit of Christian philosophy, that is, the ascetical life.[10] Finally, the solemn pursuit of her life was philosophy, understood as the love of wisdom as found in the Scriptures and in the person of Christ her Beloved, who occupied her last dying thoughts.[11]

Another woman who embodied wisdom was Marcella, a young widow in Rome, who opened her home to several virgins and widows who wished to live the ascetical life. She was renowned for her hospitality to bishops visiting from far-off regions, especially the exiled bishops of Alexandria, Athanasius and Peter. Marcella was such an ardent student of Scripture that she would pepper with questions Jerome, the young cleric who had been commissioned by Pope Damasus I to produce a good Latin translation of the Bible, known as the Vulgate. There are sixteen letters from Jerome addressed to her as responses to her queries about Scripture. Unfortunately none of her letters survive.

But one can gain a glimpse of her questions from Jerome's replies back to her. Because Jerome explains the meaning of the

---

[7] Gregory of Nyssa, *Saint Macrina*, 37.
[8] Ibid., 41.
[9] Ibid., 43.
[10] Ibid., 32.
[11] Ibid., 47.

Hebrew and Greek words of Scripture, it is highly likely that she read both languages fluently. She is so persistent in her requests for knowledge that in letters 28 and 29, Jerome refers to her as his "task-mistress" because she imposes such burdens on him to interpret the Scriptures. He would often stay up late at night researching responses and then dictate them[12] to her so they would get to her on time. One wonders what might have been the outcome of Jerome's researches on the Bible had it not been for this extraordinary woman, Marcella, in his life.

She also had a calming influence in his life in that, often, when he would write scathing treatises about people, she would remind him of the effect of his words on his hearers. Consequently, women cannot underestimate the power of their earnest questions for provoking both the hierarchy and theologians to further study, reflection, and writing on issues critical to their faith life today, just as women dared to do in the fourth century.

In letter 54.18 to the widow, Furia, Jerome held up Marcella as a model of holiness, on a par with the prophetess, Anna.

> But why should I recall instances from history and bring from books types of saintly women, when in your own city you have many before your eyes whose example you may well imitate? I shall not recount their merits here lest I should seem to flatter them. It will suffice to mention the saintly Marcella who, while she is true to the claims of her birth and station, has set before us a life which is worthy of the gospel. Anna "lived with a husband seven years from her virginity"; Marcella lived with one for seven months. Anna looked for the coming of Christ; Marcella holds fast for the Lord whom Anna received in her arms. Anna sang His praise when He was still a wailing infant; Marcella proclaims His glory now that He has won His triumph. Anna spoke of Him to those who waited for the redemption of Israel; Marcella cries out with the nations of the redeemed: "A brother redeemeth not, yet a man shall redeem,"

---

[12] J.N.D. Kelly, *Jerome: His Life, Writings, and Controversies* (New York: Harper & Row, 1975) 94–95.

and from another psalm: "A man was born in her, and the Highest Himself hath established her."[13]

Besides having a profound influence on the Scripture scholar Jerome, Marcella also served as mentor to other lovers of Scripture, Paula and her daughters, as they embraced the Christian life and undertook Bible study together and a life of prayer and fasting, while they lived in Marcella's home on the Aventine. This Paula would become Jerome's closest friend and companion when they left Rome, toured the monasteries and communities in Egypt and Palestine, and eventually settled in Bethlehem, where they established three monasteries for women and one for men. In addition to Paula and her daughters Blesilla, Eustochium, and Rufina, other women who shared in Marcella's household of faith were her mother, Albina, and Marcella's companions, Lea and Asella. From them one learns about the impact women of strong faith can have on fellow family members, friends, and associates when they gather together to share their faith with each other.

CONTEMPORARY EXAMPLES

In my own experience in a small, rural parish in southern Idaho, I would often marvel at the *ammas,* that is, the older women who listened to the cares and troubles of younger men and women struggling in their marriages, who chose to serve as "godmothers of prayer" for the junior high religion students, and never tired of providing food and support for families whose loved ones were ill or had died. This circle of women I came to rely on for support and wisdom in the parish, for they carried a long history of their families, their joys and hardships, as well as a deep love for their community, all of which made it easy for me, a young sister, asked to serve as pastoral associate and director of religious education

---

[13] Jerome, "Epistle 54," in *The Principal Works of St. Jerome,* Nicene and Post-Nicene Fathers II.vi, trans. W. H. Fremantle (Edinburgh: T & T Clark/Grand Rapids: Wm. B. Eerdmans, 1989, reprint) 108–09.

program, to call upon them when someone in the parish had a physical, emotional, or spiritual need.

I remember in particular Teresa, a grandmother, who shared with me that, one Sunday, when she had come to the parish to pray quietly, a young family came into the church with five children who were rather boisterous. And so Teresa's silence was broken by the sounds of the children. As she started to complain to her Lord that she wanted to spend a few quiet moments in his presence, she heard the words in her heart, "These are my children. Can you pray for them?" From this she began a practice in which she would come to the parish before Mass, either on Sunday or during the week, sit in the pew, and wait for whoever God presented in the pew in front of her. She would offer prayer for them. She told me that the amazing thing that happened to her as she practiced this mindfulness is that they ceased to be troublesome to her thoughts. They became, as it were, blessings of God in her life.

Another woman in the parish whom I appreciated was Betty, the parish organist. I was in the parish but two weeks when she came to me and said, "Sister Mary, I am going to pray for you every day." I replied, "Well, Betty, what a precious gift; thank you very much." She continued, "I am going to pray for the fruitfulness of your work in the parish." Again I thanked her. The last year I was in the parish, three years later, one of the last things I attended was Betty's funeral. The church was packed. The pastor got up and said at the homily: "We all know of the suffering that was part of Betty's life these last months. But there is something none of you know because she only shared it with me the last night before she died."

When Betty was a young woman and organist in the parish, her husband left her, and eventually they were divorced. That was very much a scandal to someone in the 1940s. She, of course, suffered the effects of that scandal in terms of being ostracized by some members of the parish and even some of her own relatives. One day she went to the church, sat before the Blessed Sacrament, and said to Jesus: "I do not know how to carry this burden." She heard a voice in her heart say to her: "Betty, can you come and spend an hour with me every day and intercede for every member of this parish?" She replied in the affirmative. She did that for the rest of her life. Of course, there was not a dry eye in the church when the pastor revealed her hidden intercession. Then I recalled Betty's words about praying for me. Little did I know the power of that woman's prayer and her witness to us in the parish.

REFLECTION EXERCISE

I invite you to take some time and consider two or three biblical texts that have served as living words in your life. Or a time when Jesus spoke words that empowered your faith. Think about those words and who you have become, because God has written these words on your heart. How have your attitudes changed? How have these words been a source of consolation or conversion in your life? Or you may wish to reflect on those with whom you regularly share insights from Scripture. Who would you say is the network of faithful friends who deepen your understanding of the Bible and of the philosophy of the living word of God?

FURTHER SCRIPTURAL PASSAGES FOR PRAYER

Psalm 119:81-112	God's Word is salvific
Isaiah 40:1-8	Promise of salvation
Matthew 26:36-45	Waiting with the Lord in the Garden of Gethsemane
Acts 2:42-47	The communal life
Romans 8:14-17, 26-27	God's children praying in the Spirit

3   Heralds in the Desert

OPENING REFLECTION: Luke 3:1a, 2b-6, 15-18

O God of John the Baptist, herald of good news, with what great power you spoke through your servant John, in order to arouse the people to the immediacy of allowing their hearts to be pierced with the fire of your word. Let our hearts be set aflame during our times of prayer and silence this day, that we may experience "making ready the way of the Lord" this day. We ask this in the name of the One who baptizes us in the Holy Spirit and in fire, Jesus Christ our Lord. Amen.

INTRODUCTORY REMARKS

One image of John the Baptist is that of a fierce ascetical figure—gaunt with fasting, yet eyes piercing with the discerning insight into the condition of one's soul, which is not always a soothing image to contemplate. That image is influenced by the rail-thin, goatskin-clad figure of John that stands at the entryway to the Abbey Church of Saint John the Baptist in Collegeville, Minnesota. The desert is a harsh climate in which to dwell and one would have to be called to be a herald of its truth.

The desert for the *ammas* and *abbas* of the fourth and fifth centuries was a rather ambivalent place and expression.[1] Early in

---

[1] Antoine Guillaumont, *Aux origenes du monachisme chrétien: Pour une phéno-ménologie du monachisme*, Spiritualité orientale, 30 (Maine & Loire: Abbaye de Bellefontaine, 1979) 69.

28

the Bible, there was an idealism or mystique associated with the desert because it was the place where the Israelites spent forty years, a place where God made a covenant with them. To the Hebrew prophets, a return to the desert was the sign of reconciliation with YHWH.[2] There is another association that is far more realistic. All peoples of the ancient Near East viewed the desert as the complete opposite of inhabited and cultivated land; the desert was a deserted and sterile land, often associated with the devastations of war or, in the case of the Israelites, the curse of Yahweh, for it was there all manner of savage beasts lived. Moreover, in the Egyptian mind, the desert was the dwelling place of demons.[3]

However, in the literature of the first century before Christ and continuing into the first centuries of the Christian era, there was a Hellenistic notion that provided a romantic nuance to desert as a place of solitude, to which the weary person of the city could retire in order to regain peace and involve oneself in philosophy or meditation. The close association of the Greek words *heremos* [`ερημοζ] and *heremia* [ἐρημία] (meaning "desert") with *hē remia* [ηρεμία] (meaning "calm") probably accounts for this notion. Accordingly, Origen refers to John the Baptist's enjoyment of the calm life and solitude of the desert[4] where he combines both of these ideas. This sense of solitude and retirement is used by Basil of Caesarea in his letter 14 (ca. 360) to his friend Gregory of Nazianzen, the former trying to persuade the latter to join him in his monastic project at Annesi.[5]

Jerome, too, in his early days of solitude in the desert of Chalcis, Syria, will write enthusiastically of the desert to his friend Heliodorus: "O desert, bright with the flowers of Christ! O solitude whence come the stones of which, in the Apocalypse, the

[2] Ibid., 69–70.

[3] Ibid., 70.

[4] Ibid., 73–74, citing Origen, *Homélies sur Luc* XI and X (ed. Crouzel, Fournier and Périchon, Paris, 1962); cf. *Homélies sur l'Exode*, III.3 (trad. Fortier et de Lubac, Paris, 1947).

[5] Guillaumont, *Aux origenes du monachisme chrétien*, 74–75.

city of the great king is built! O wilderness, gladdened with God's especial presence! What keeps you in the world, my brother, you who are above the world? How long shall gloomy roofs oppress you? How long shall smoky cities immure you? Believe me, I have more light than you. Sweet it is to lay aside the weight of the body and soar into the pure bright ether."[6]

In fact, Jerome could only stand the Chalcis desert a couple of years, for his health failed from harsh fasting. He became em-broiled in the disputes over how to express the mystery of the Trinity, part of the controversies that were raging in the East. Moreover, his was a very difficult personality, described by the scholar, J.N.D. Kelly, as "self-willed and sharp-tongued, irascible . . . inordinately proud of his Roman links," which would only have heightened the uneasy relations he had with his unculti-vated, less-educated, Syriac-speaking neighbors.[7]

In Jerome's *Life of Paul*, a fictitious work modeled on the *Life of Antony*,[8] the desert was portrayed as a place inhabited by strange and sympathetic animals, as well as a place of miracles.[9] This kind of writing would generate an enduring literary picture of the desert as the place where God dwells,[10] as the scene of battles of heroic monastic men and women with the demons of human passions, and as the paradise regained where humans and beasts dwell in idyllic harmony.

---

[6] Jerome, "Letter 14.10," in *St. Jerome: Letters and Select Works, Nicene and Post-Nicene Fathers* 2.6, trans. W. H. Fremantle (Edinburgh: T & T Clark/Grand Rapids, Mich.: Wm. B. Eerdmans, 1989, reprint) 17.

[7] J.N.D. Kelly, *Jerome: His Life, Writings and Controversies* (New York: Harper & Row, Publishers, 1975) 48 and 52 on his fasting, 52–53 on the Trinitar-ian controversies, and 55 on aspects of his personality.

[8] This is the position taken by Manfred Fuhrmann, "Die Mönchsgeschichten des Hieronymus Form-experimente in erzählender Literatur," *Christianisme et formes littéraires de l'antiquité tardive en occident*, Fondation Hardt pour l'étude de l'antiquité classique entretiens, 23 (Geneva: Fondation Hardt, 1977) 41–99.

[9] Guillaumont, *Aux origenes du monachisme chrétien*, 76.

[10] Ibid., 76.

STORIES AND COMMENTARY

The *amma* who immediately comes to mind as a strong recluse of the desert is Amma Sarah. The very first apophthegm or wise saying attributed to her reveals her battle with lust. "It was related of Amma Sarah that for thirteen years she waged warfare against the demon of fornication. She never prayed that the warfare should cease but she said, 'O God, give me strength.'"[11] Sarah seems to be a stronger character than even Saint Paul. Whereas he had prayed three times to have the "thorn in his flesh" be removed (2 Cor 12:7-8) and received only the reply, "My strength is enough for you, for in weakness power reaches perfection" (2 Cor 12:9), Sarah never even prayed for the removal of her temptation. She trusted that God would hear her request for strength and it was given her. That God provided the grace is revealed in the second apophthegm, which states "Once the same spirit of fornication attacked her more insistently, reminding her of the vanities of the world. But she gave herself up to the fear of God and to asceticism and went up onto her little terrace to pray. Then the spirit of fornication appeared corporally to her and said, 'Sarah, you have overcome me.' But she said, 'It is not I who have overcome you, but my master, Christ.'"[12]

This profound sense of knowing from where came the grace to overcome her inner struggle with the thoughts is an example of humility. She held God so reverently in her awareness, that is, the fear of God was so much a part of her being, that she ceased to be afraid of the visitations of temptations, relying on that same God to protect her. She never swayed from her monastic observances or her prayer to this God who provided in the midst of her struggle.

---

[11] "Sarah #1," in *The Sayings of the Desert Fathers: The Alphabetical Collection*, Cistercian Studies 59, trans. Benedicta Ward (London & Oxford: Mowbray/ U.S.A.: Cistercian Publications, 1975) 229.

[12] "Sarah #2," in *The Sayings of the Desert Fathers*, 230.

One witnesses here a woman who was strengthened in the desert through battles with temptations that she knew her Lord had conquered. He was her guide, master, and wisdom for her own journey into holiness by means of these battles. And these fights with the demons won for her a reputation among the *abbas* of the desert, as yet another apophthegm reveals. "Another time, two old men, great anchorites, came to the district of Pelusia to visit her. When they arrived one said to the other, 'Let us humiliate this old woman.' So they said to her, 'Be careful not to become conceited thinking to yourself: "Look how anchorites are coming to see me, a mere woman."' But Amma Sarah said to them, 'According to nature I am a woman, but not according to my thoughts.'"[13]

What Sarah's clever retort reveals is the wordplay common in the region of that time. She recognizes that she is in fact a woman by virtue of birth, but not by virtue of God's grace operating in her thoughts. In other words, she became virtuous, or virile ("manly" in the idiom of that time), "by direct action, by 'fighting' . . . [her] nature became equal" to that of men because, as Palladius records, there were "certain women with many qualities to whom God apportioned labours equal to those of men, lest any should pretend that women are too feeble to practise virtue perfectly" (LH 41).[14] Unlike some women ascetics, who hid their female identity by shaving off their hair and wearing the garments of men in order to avoid potential rape by brigands, Sarah retained her own identity. As a consequence, she came under a more rigorous scrutiny and testing of her vocation from the very co-members of the ascetical life that she had undertaken.[15]

Her testing by fire was rewarded with gifts from God, which were not always known to her directly. A little known apophthegm tells of "a layman who had mocked Amma Sara when he saw her crossing a brook, [and] was killed by a single word pronounced

[13] "Sarah #4," in *The Sayings of the Desert Fathers*, 230.

[14] Gillian Cloke, *The Female Man of God: Women and Spiritual Power in the Patristic Age, AD 350–450* (London & New York: Routledge, 1995) 214.

[15] Ibid., 198.

unconsciously by the moniale. But a simple prayer immediately obtained the return to life of the disrespectful man: 'My Jesus, bring him back to life, and from now on I won't ever utter such words again.' The narrator says that Sara 'was not aware of the grace of God residing in her.'"[16]

The desert for monastic athletes like Sarah was a real and fearsome thing in Egypt. Egyptian *fellahs*, or peasants, who predominantly lived in the villages along the Nile or in the Delta region, considered the desert a place of terror. Their lives in the oases were boundaried by the great deserts around them—the Libyan Desert to the west and the more mountainous Arabic Desert to the east. The Nile area was called *kémi*, or "black land," dedicated to the god of life, Osiris, and his son, Horus, who was posed against Seth, the god of the sterile desert, or the "red land," who was hostile and malevolent.[17]

The desert was not only sterile, but also "the region of the tombs, the domain of the dead, where the Egyptian never ventured without fear."[18] It was the area of bands of nomads who were often hostile to strangers. Moreover, the desert was home to such dangerous animals as serpents, hyenas, snakes, and jackals that inhabited its abandoned temples and ruins.[19] No better description of this desert exists than that of the *Life of Antony* (chapters 12, 50–52), as a wilderness of wild beasts, creeping things, and demons.

Soon so many monks and a few virgins came to dwell in the desert that it became a veritable city. The term *desertum ciuitas* (the desert a city) acquired two meanings. First, the deserts became literally peopled with hundreds of monks, many of them living in lauras or associations of huts and cells. Eventually,

---

[16] Lucien Regnault, *The Day-to-Day Life of the Desert Fathers in Fourth-Century Egypt*, trans. Étienne Poirier, Jr. (Petersham, Mass.: St. Bede's, 1999) 221.

[17] Guillaumont, *Aux origenes du monachisme chrétien*, 77.

[18] Ibid., 77–78.

[19] Ibid., 78.

monasteries arose to accommodate the growing numbers and gardens were planted to provide food for the many guests who came.[20] Secondly, in a spiritual sense, the desert was the place of ascetical combat where the devil had come to tempt Christ. As the monastic scholar Antoine Guillaumont has pointed out, "This scene points to the victory of Christ over Satan, which inaugurates a redemptive work. In this perspective, the monk, by going to the desert to do battle against the devil and to triumph over him, reproduces, continues in a certain manner, the redemptive action. Thus [s/]he is an 'athlete', who goes to the desert in order to confront the demons, in order to battle with them . . . in the open and eye to eye."[21]

Thus we see that Sarah was among those athletes; she was revered enough by the early monastic tradition that the sayings about her "manly" virtue were committed orally to memory and then eventually written down. She, like John the Baptist, could speak the truth in love and exhibited a profound humility about the source of her inner power. Both were heralds of God's life proclaimed in witness of the One who was greater—the Master—whose sandal John was not worthy to untie and whose example Sarah emulated in her own ascetical observance.

CONTEMPORARY EXAMPLE

In my own life as a young sister, one of the demons I struggled with was the demon of anger, the passion of anger, or the compulsion of anger. These are all expressions for talking about what ancients called the vices. A sister in my community came to me one day and said, "Mary, if you don't do something about your anger, we don't know how you are going to live with us in community." That was a profound moment of humility for me. I remember weeping for quite some time, for I said to God, "I don't

[20] Ibid., 80–81.
[21] Ibid., 81.

know what to do about this." In typical Mary-fashion, I went to our library and checked out every book and article we had on anger, and I read all twenty-three of them. It took me a while. After I read the books, I could describe anger in practically every manifestation that there was, but it was not cured.

Fortunately, a couple of years later, a retreat directress came to the monastery whose theme for the retreat was "Fear, Anger and Sexual Energy—The Three Struggles of Women Religious." After her first conference on anger, I knew that I had to go see that lady. I was the first to sign up to put my check mark on the sheet on the conference room door. I brought my little list of the twenty-three books and articles I had read when I went in to talk with her. I sat down and shared with Sister Jeanne what the sister had said to me and how I was still struggling with this. I said, "Here is the list of twenty-three books and articles. Do you want to see it?" I still remember the look on her face. She had this wonderful twinkle in her eye, and there was the start of a quiver in her mouth. It was as if she wanted to smile but did not dare because I was quite serious about this matter. She said, "No, Mary, I don't need to see the list. But I want you to consider something. What if anger is merely a signpost that something is going on in your heart and in your life? Can you learn to read it as a signal that God is trying to tell you something more about your anger than you know at this time?" I just looked at her. She continued, "Can you let anger be your friend?" I answered, "Well, I've tried everything else. I guess I can try that."

And so from that day forward I have been learning how to read the signs of anger. I have been learning that underneath the anger, God has been revealing to me my profound capacity for a sense of justice, or a capacity to name manipulation, or a sense of when I am in great need. I have not been listening to that, the times in which I have been feeling jealous or fearful and anger masks that, and the times I have felt depressed and not let myself be aware of that. Anger over the years has revealed to me a variety of ways of being. I thank God for Sister Jeanne in my life.

I met her again two years ago and told her, "You have been the instrument of God's leading me on a pathway about this passion I never knew was possible." This struggle has taught me that the desert is that place where God speaks to our heart and transforms the vital energy that has been a pain in our life into the gift of gold that lies underneath.

REFLECTION EXERCISE

I invite you today to reflect on God's power and strength working in you, and how that ever-faithful God has brought you to this time and place in your life. You may wish to ponder how God's word has been a sword piercing your self-understanding and calling you to ever-deeper reverence and awe, so that you have been able to do infinitely more than you ever thought or imagined you could. Or you may wish to consider a time in your life when God was very near, so near that you thought God was absent and all the while God sustained your vocation, your struggle, your time of trial with persevering stability, loving mercy, and sustaining courage. A few passages are listed below which you may wish to pray over as you reflect on God's heralding strength in weakness, courage in the face of opposition, and mercy in time of overwhelming temptation.

FURTHER SCRIPTURAL PASSAGES FOR PRAYER

Luke 3:1-6, 15-18	Preaching of John the Baptist
2 Corinthians 12:1-10	God's grace is sufficient
Ephesians 3:14-21	Prayer for the community
Colossians 1:15-23	Preeminence of Christ and his work

4   Desert as Idyllic Garden

OPENING REFLECTION: Isaiah 11:1-4, 6-9

O Spirit of the Lord, rest on us this day, as we ponder the mystery of the vision you hold out to us. It seems impossible that a wolf and lamb, a leopard and kid, a calf and young lion, could be play-mates, let alone a child place its hand in an adder's lair and not be harmed. And yet you call each of us to reconcile whatever lamb and wolf, kid and leopard, lion and calf are represented by aspects of our own personalities, so that we in turn can believe it possible for humans to live in peace with each other in our world. Show us the way of this just rule of your reign in our hearts, that we may be instruments of that reign wherever you send us. We ask this in your name Immanuel, God-with-us. Amen.

INTRODUCTORY REMARKS

In the last chapter the aspect of desert that was addressed was the battleground for growing in virtue. While a few ascetics may have gone to the desert to battle the demons, far more sought to find God there. In the desert, the monastic sought to unify one's life, that is, to renounce whatever was the source of division. To do so meant abandoning the pursuit of land, the life of the village, and the accumulation of possessions. The desert represented a rupture from the "world"; it was a place far from the attachment to the cares and goods of the world. Thus "flight into the desert" became flight from the responsibilities toward the land, daily contacts with people, especially the opposite gender, in order to pursue *hesychia*—solitude, tranquility, and the practice of continual remembrance of God. The attraction of this pursuit drew many to the desert and made of it eventually a city.[1]

However, solitude did not mean an immediate freedom from all temptations and distractions. In the desert, the monastic person strove in a battle of his/her heart against the *logismoi*—the passions of gluttony, lust, anger, avarice, sadness, *acedia*, vainglory, and pride—that manifested themselves in nostalgic memories of past luxuries and relationships. Solitude meant facing the daily assaults of discouragement, lethargy, and other subtle underminings of one's observances and commitment to God. Over long years, the heart became quieted and stilled to welcome pure prayer and the experience of the Divine One who dwells in the heart.[2]

STORIES AND COMMENTARY

One of the women who struggled with her passions and by the grace of God was transformed into an icon of God's presence was Mary of Egypt. Mary was the main character of the fable in the Introduction, the penitent woman who encountered Zossima, the monk who was seeking someone holier than himself. After Zossima and Mary had their conversation that first Lent, she begged him not to reveal anything of which they spoke, sending him off with the words:

---

[1] Antoine Guillaumont, *Aux origenes du monachisme chrétien: Pour une phénoménologie du monachisme*, Spiritualité orientale, 30 (Maine & Loire: Abbaye de Bellefontaine, 1979) 83–84.

[2] Ibid., 85–86. For a helpful explanation of the process by which the *logismoi*, that is, impure thoughts *(Logismoi akatharoi)* or those leading to the passions, from a beginning suggestion all the way to formation of a vicious habit, see Tomáš Špidlík, *The Spirituality of the Christian East: A Systematic Handbook*, Cistercian Studies 79, trans. Anthony P. Gythiel (Kalamazoo: Cistercian Publications, 1986) 238–41.

"Go in peace, and this time next year I will show myself again to
you, and you will see me, if God preserves us. And for the Lord's
sake, do what I am going to ask: when the holy season of fasting
comes round next year, do not cross the Jordan as is usually done
in that monastery. . . . Stay in the monastery, father, as I have
told you, and even if you want to go out, you will not be able to do
so. But at sunset on the most holy day of the Lord's Supper, take
for me a portion of the life-giving Body and Blood in a holy vessel,
worthy of such mysteries, and bring it to me on the bank of Jordan, on the inhabited side, so that when I come I may receive the
life-giving gifts. Since the time when I made my communion in the
church of the most blessed Forerunner before crossing the Jordan,
never have I received those holy things, and so I implore you not to
refuse my request: bring me the life-giving and divine mysteries at
that hour when the Lord made His disciples partakers of the holy
Supper. . . ." With these words, she asked him to pray for her,
and disappeared very swiftly into the depths of the desert.[3]

Mary had lived in the desert in complete solitude for forty-seven
years, weeping for her past sinful life and knowing the Lord was
teaching her the truth of the Scriptures within her heart, although
she had no Bible of her own to read. This inner communion nour-
ished her, even when the sacred elements were not available to
her. But she did wish to receive Christ in Eucharist and so she
asked that favor of Zossima. He, in turn, honored her request to
tell no one of his extraordinary visit with her. He could hardly
wait for the year to roll around to Lent. That Lent, sure enough
as Mary's prophecy had foretold, he was unable to leave the monastery, so overcome by a fever was he. Recuperating before Holy
Thursday, he took a portion of the precious Body and Blood of
Christ in a small chalice, as well as some figs and dates in a bas-
ket and a few lentils soaked in water for his friend. He sat on the
bank of the River Jordan, the same river where John the Forerunner had baptized Jesus, and waited. He waited a long time, so

[3] Benedicta Ward, "St Mary of Egypt; the Liturgical Icon of Repentance," in
Harlots of the Desert: A Study in Repentance in Early Monastic Sources (London
& Oxford: Mowbray, 1987) ch. 20, pp. 51–52.

long in fact that he began to weep out of loss that he might have missed her. In the midst of his tears, she came walking on the water toward him. When asked for a blessing, he blessed her, then prayed the Creed and the Lord's Prayer, and she gave him the sign of peace, after which she received the Eucharist. Her prayer of thanksgiving was that of Simeon's on seeing Jesus in the Temple, "Lord, now let your servant depart in peace, according to your word; for my eyes have seen your salvation" (Luke 2:29). Once again, she asked Zossima to return the following year on Holy Thursday. When he wanted to give her the food he had brought, she deigned to take three grains of lentils, in honor of the Trinity, and then asked for his prayers for herself, a sinner. He dropped to her feet and wept copiously, begging her for her prayers for the church and for himself.[4]

This story is full of allusions to Christ, but what is profoundly amazing is that the Christ-figure is Mary the reformed harlot. It is she who walks on water to her disciple Zossima, who waits on the bank of the river with food for her soul and her body. The Lord's Prayer joins them together in community, preparatory to receiving the sacred Body and Blood of Christ. And it is Zossima, like the repentant woman, who weeps over the feet of Mary, the embodiment of Christ in his life. Moreover, she gives him the sign of peace.

A year later, he returned to the desert, once again with the sacred Body and Blood of Christ. He waited quite a long time, but Mary did not come. Finally, with a face full of tears, he prayed to God to show him "the angel in the flesh." In answer to the prayer, Zossima walked to a stream, on the other side of which he saw her body, with hands folded and her face turned eastward. Immediately, "he watered the feet of the blessed one with tears." Then he saw a message in the sand that read "Father Zossima, bury in this place the body of Mary the sinner, return me to the earth of which I am made, dust to dust, having prayed to the Lord for

[4]Ibid., chs. 21–22, 52–54.

me, who died on the first day of the Egyptian month of Pharmuti called the fifth of the Ides of April by the Romans, on the self-same night as the Passion of the Lord after making her communion of the Divine and Mysterious Supper."[5]

He deeply desired to honor her request to bury her, but he had no tools with which to dig her a grave, having only his hands. He saw a small stick and set to digging the grave with it, but it was much too small for the hard ground and he soon grew tired. Looking up he noticed

> a huge lion standing by the body of the Holy One and licking her feet. When he saw the lion he trembled with fear, especially because he remembered that Mary said she had never met any animals. But protecting himself with the sign of the cross, he believed that he would be kept from harm by the power of the One who lay there. As for the lion, it walked up to him, expressing friendliness in every movement. Zossima said to the lion, "Greatest of the beasts, you have been sent by God, so that the body of the Holy One should be buried, for I am old and have not enough strength to dig her grave. I have no spade and I cannot go back all that distance to fetch suitable tools. So do the work with your paws and we shall be able to give to the earth the mortal tabernacle of the saint."

> While he was still speaking the lion had already dug out with its front paws a hole big enough to bury the body in. Again the old man watered the feet of the Holy One with tears and then, with the lion standing by, he called upon her to pray for everyone, he covered her body with the earth; it was naked as it had been before, except for the torn monastic cloak which Zossima had thrown across her and with which Mary, turning away, had partially covered her body. Then they both withdrew. The lion went off into the depths of the desert as meekly if it were a lamb, and Zossima went home, blessing and praising God and singing hymns of praise to our Lord Christ.[6]

As in a number of female saints' lives, the death of the saint serves as a moment of recognition in a form of double ascent: the saint mounts to heaven and the world gains knowledge of her

[5] Ibid., ch. 25, 54–55.
[6] Ibid., chs. 26–27, 55–56.

identity. This is clearly seen in the story of Mary of Egypt for, although Zossima knows her history, he does not know her name "until he finds her body with the injunction written beside it" to bury her.[7] In accounts of death and recognition, words for knowing are common. Thus Zossima rejoices that Mary has taught *(didicit)* him her name. This kind of "vocabulary suggests that disguise also is a motif of descent, a step on the downward journey that will ultimately lead to ascent, recognition, knowledge, conversion, union with Christ. Disguise . . . displace[s] death in which the hero, having shed an old identity, assumes an interim one prior to the final moment of revelation with which comes the integration of past and present."[8] She ascends into the eternal present with Christ.

In the journey of a saint, "rivers are potent symbols of change, as seen by the prominence in rituals such as baptism."[9] At the beginning of her journey, Mary had washed herself in the river Jordan prior to her eating the bread of Communion with the Lord and crossing over the river to the deeper desert. In the section above, Mary walked on the water to Zossima for their visit.

Zossima's journey is one of finding someone beyond him in deeds, which will help him learn that there are many roads to salvation.[10] The search for this other takes him beyond the confines of his known world and exposes him to greater trials than he had ever experienced. "What he eventually finds in the desert is both a woman and knowledge; he finds St. Mary the Egyptian,"[11] and he learns that she is one greater than he in virtue.

Another key element in this spiritual fantasy tale is the eschatological hope for the return of the Lost Paradise, "'the miraculous time when man existed in friendship with the beasts.' The object

[7] Alison Goddard Elliott, *Roads to Paradise: Reading the Lives of the Early Saints* (Hanover & London: Published for Brown University Press by University Press of New England, 1987) 119.

[8] Ibid., 120.
[9] Ibid., 122.
[10] Ibid., 125.
[11] Ibid., 126.

of this solitary quest is to atone for Adam's sin by living in imitation of the new Adam, and thereby to regain the lost Golden Age of Eden."[12] In patristic literature, Paradise was seen as the goal of every Christian. The desert saints manifested the universal inner and spiritual quest for this Paradise in outward and symbolic ways.[13] The desert came to represent the place where the male or female monk recaptured the lost human nature. "Three characteristic practices unite the seekers of 'paradise for the soul' in the desert": 1) arduous fasting coupled with other forms of mortification and denial of creature comforts; 2) virginity; and 3) power over beasts, particularly lions. Posed in these stories was the rejection of civilization, represented by cooked food and the pursuit of a life consistent with nature (raw) as spiritually defined.[14] Consequently, most desert hermits were portrayed as vegetarians.

For some early monastic writers, fasting was interpreted as "atonement for Adam's fall," because the original sin was considered to be gluttony.[15] "As gluttony expelled the one who ruled from Paradise, so abstinence has recalled the one who has gone astray to Paradise," according to Ambrose.[16] In addition, monastic writers like John Cassian maintained that fasting was necessary to repress sexual desire.[17] So Mary of Egypt was portrayed as living for seventeen years in the desert on two and one-half loaves of bread and on grass, for to eat anything else was to have inflamed her passions.[18]

The final characteristic that marked the saint as different from ordinary folks was his/her rapport with animals. Most frequently, the king of beasts is associated with desert fathers and mothers.[19] This association comes partly from the imagery of the symbols

[12] Ibid., 133.
[13] Ibid., 136.
[14] Ibid., 137.
[15] Ibid., 140.
[16] Ibid., 141.
[17] Ibid., 141.
[18] Ibid., 142.
[19] Ibid., 144.

for the Gospels in which the lion represents the Gospel of Mark, whose first words are about a voice crying in the desert. In early Christian literature the lion represented resurrection.[20]

Although the early Christians were thrown to the lions in the Coliseum, early *acta* accounts of martyrs were more likely to have the beast run up to the saints, fall in reverence before them and lick their feet.[21] The Acts of Thecla represented this kind of portrayal in which a lioness protected the saint, bowed at her feet, and gave up its life in defense of her.[22] A common detail in saints' lives was that the animal sent to kill them came and licked the soles of their feet or their wounds in a healing fashion. Behind these clichés lay "a consistent vision of the significance of the animals' behavior," which pointed to "a reversal of codes, a change of nature." The beast refused to act in a bestial way, whereas the tyrant persecuting the saint acted like a beast.[23] It is as if the animal remembered what humans have forgotten: the majesty of God revealed in the holy one. The lion or other ferocious beasts might enhance this image by going away gentle as a lamb,[24] as the lion did in the story of Mary's burial.

The precedent in the Bible for such dominion over lions is the story of Daniel (chapters 6 and 14),[25] which was one of the most popular tales in early Christianity used as an image of liberation and a symbol of resurrection. While Daniel claimed innocence and purity as the reasons for his escape, the early Church writers pointed to his safety being connected to his fasting, according to Ambrose and Basil, or due to his chastity, according to John Damascene.[26]

---

[20] Ibid., 145.
[21] Ibid., 146.
[22] Ibid., 148.
[23] Ibid., 149.
[24] Ibid., 150.
[25] Ibid., 152.
[26] Ibid., 152–53; cf. Ambrose, *Liber de Elia et ieiunio*, PL 14,704B and John Damascene, *De fide orthodoxa* IV,24, in Patrologia Graeca 94, 1210A.

The imagery of the gentle lion burying the saint represents a parallel movement in the animal's life that one has seen in the life of the saint: a return to the original state.[27] "Power over lions in the Hebrew, Christian and Arab traditions, is the 'touchstone of sanctity and purity.'" Especially for Christians, the lion represents Christ in Revelation 5:5, the one who executes the divine will.[28] Moreover, the gentleness of the lion-turned-lamb is a portrayal of the coming of the Messiah, foretold in Isaiah 11:6, in which the wolf will lie down with the lamb and the leopard with the kid; the calf and young lion will be together and a little child will lead them.[29]

Early Christian writers loaded the stories of their saintly heroes and heroines with biblical images so that the audience receiving these stories would immediately recognize texts learned by heart, see themselves in the stories and take to heart the message of God's redemptive care of sinners. Mary's story is one of many reversals: a redeemed prostitute becomes as Christ to a holy monk, who has yet to learn the humility of real sanctity—that all depends on God and naught on the holiness of one's own making; the desert becomes an Eden where the waters of the great river prefigure baptism; the great lion is a servant-lamb who washes the feet of the saint with his tongue, while her disciple weeps over her feet in humble recognition of who she really is.

CONTEMPORARY EXAMPLE

Beasts acting gently as lambs reminds me of an incident a number of years ago. A companion and I were out walking a country road and stopped by a pasture to talk for a few moments. All of a sudden there was a ferocious sound coming from the end of the pasture. A donkey, with teeth bared and braying for all he was worth, was running from the end of the pasture toward us.

[27] Elliott, *Roads to Paradise*, 165.
[28] Ibid., 167.
[29] Ibid.

I stepped back onto the road, while my companion reached over the fence and scratched the ears and nose of the donkey, which looked at her as if he were in ecstasy! My friend is a lover of animals and, although the two of them had never met, it seemed that the donkey knew my companion's gentle spirit.

REFLECTION EXERCISE

I invite you to be with the passage from Isaiah 11:1-4a, 6-9. You may wish to ask the Spirit to guide you to your own desert, where the Lord awaits you in the desire to transform it into paradise. What wolf, leopard, or lion threatens your sense of safety but, when dialogued with in the presence of the Holy One, holds the possibility of transformation into a lamb, calf, or kid—gentle images of God's mercy, compassion, and humility? Where might God visit you in the efforts you have made to draw close to divine love? Let the Lord Immanuel, whose vision Isaiah proclaimed, draw you there this day, as God wills and directs.

FURTHER SCRIPTURAL PASSAGES FOR PRAYER

Isaiah 65:17-25   The world renewed
Daniel 6:11-25   Daniel in the lions' den
Luke 15:1-7   Parable of the lost sheep
John 10:1-18   The Good Shepherd
Revelation 5:1-14   The scroll and the lamb

5   The Pearl of Great Price

OPENING REFLECTION: Matthew 13:44-46

O God of treasures and of fine pearls, what would it be like to find such a treasure this day! Yet that is precisely how you look on each of us—as a pearl worth giving your life on behalf of. Teach us what it means to be so cherished by you that we in turn know more deeply how to treasure each other as pearls of great price, gifts of your unique image and likeness each one. We ask this in your holy name, Jesus Christ, our Lord. Amen.

INTRODUCTORY REMARKS

The pearl of great price is an image that is a favorite one for the hagiographer of Amma Syncletica's life. For many centuries the only thing known about this desert *amma*, who lived near Alexandria in the late fourth to early fifth century, is that her sayings were collected and added to the *Sayings of the Desert Fathers* in the fifth century. Only within the past century was her life translated into French and then into English, so that in some circles she is becoming more widely known.[1] Her life is disap-

---

[1] The French translation of this life is *Vie de Sainte Synclétique et Discours de salut d'une vierge*, Spiritualité Orientale 9, trans. Odile Bénédicte Bernard and J. Bouvet (Abbaye Notre-Dame de Bellefontaine, 1972). The best English translation is found in Pseudo-Athanasius, *The Life of the Blessed & Holy Syncletica*, Part One, trans. Elizabeth Bryson Bongie; Part Two: *A Study of the Life* is by Mary Schaffer (Toronto: Peregrina, 2001).

pointing from the point of view of history, for we learn hardly anything at all about her background, other than she was born in Macedonia of fairly wealthy Christian parents and the family migrated to Alexandria, Egypt, in order to live more closely among Christians. She had two brothers, one of whom died in childhood and the other died just before his marriage, and one blind sister.[2] Her life, according to the legend that has come down to us, was written in order to show a feminine counterpart to Antony, the great desert hermit.

Syncletica is presented as a precocious child from the fact that she took up prayer and fasting at an early age. Of course, hagiographers are fond of pointing to early signs of a vocation by highlighting ascetical practices begun in youth. Anyway, after her parents' death, she took her blind sister with her to the tomb of a relative outside of Alexandria in order to live a life of poverty and dedication to God. This experience at the tombs is to be understood as a parallel with Antony's experience of living in the cave in the inner desert. That is, she was living a life of solitude, dedicated to prayer and communion with God as a virgin: "This shutting up of oneself in the solitary confinement of a sepulchre for the purpose of meditation had been practiced in pagan Egypt by the priests at the service of the god Serapis who lived in the Serapeum temple at Memphis. The practice of visiting the tombs was considered an experience of 'living death': one approached the likeness to death and from there journeyed to the 'frontiers of the beyond' in the hope of arriving at a secret, hidden understanding."[3]

How long Syncletica lived this solitary life is uncertain, but one day other women found her and asked her to teach them how

[2] Bongie, "Introduction," *The Life of Syncletica*, 5. Hereafter all references to the actual text of the life will be indicated in the body of the text as VS, followed by paragraph number.

[3] Mary Forman, "Amma Syncletica—A Spirituality of Experience," in *On Pilgrimage: The Best of Ten Years of Vox Benedictina*, ed. Margot King (Toronto, Ont.: Peregrina Publications, 1994) 262–63, with quotations taken from Jacques Lacarriere, *Men Possessed by God*, trans. Roy Monkcom (Garden City: Doubleday, 1964) 216.

to live a holy life. Although she was at first reluctant to do so, she gave way to their persuasion for learning how to seek God, and she agreed to share from her own experience how to discern the movements of the spirit within; "her words [were] nothing other than the distillation of the way she lived."[4] The basis for her life was a profound love of God and neighbor. The major portion of her *vita*, or *Life*, is actually a large collection of her teaching that she shared with the women who came to live with her in some form of communal life in Alexandria.

The schema for Syncletica's life and teaching was discovered by Mary Schaffer, who became enchanted by the story of Syncletica and her wisdom. Mary sought to find a coherent structure in the text so as to understand why this life would have been read in the early centuries of feminine monasticism, but somehow was described by twentieth-century translators of the text as badly written. As Mary did *lectio* on the text for months at a time she discovered that the text and its teaching had its own inherent structure[5] that does not yield itself to a single or even ten-fold reading.

STORIES AND COMMENTARY

One of the discoveries Mary made was that the whole of this life is centered on the parable of the precious pearl, the same passage that opened this chapter. The unknown author of the *Life* offered this clue to its meaning in the following words:

> There is a need for all people to live their lives with a knowledge of what is good. For if they are thus trained in the practical aspects [of living], they possess in life something with no liens attached and, moreover, much of what is beneficial escapes the notice of those with less experience. They suffer this disadvantage as a result of the entrenchment of a perspective blurred through negligence. For often pearls of great price go unrecognized by poor men, and those

---

[4] Schaffer, *The Life of the Blessed and Holy Syncletica*, Part Two, 20.
[5] Ibid., 39.

inexperienced in the working of these precious gems scorn them as something small and of no value (VS 1).

In other words, the pursuit of holiness demands the practice of observances, which, to the uninitiated and ignorant, is of no benefit because they suffer from the blindness of their own perceptions, which serve as a form of the truth for them. Thus they miss the "precious gems" that living the life holds in store. Also, the author tells the reader that one will only come to the knowledge that leads to contemplation in stages, much like the formation of a pearl happens in stages or layers.

Thus Syncletica's life and teaching are revealed to be a pearl—that is, the pearl is the central image and symbol of the spiritual message contained in the work itself.[6] All wisdom for Syncletica is located in the Gospel of Jesus Christ. When one is in search of the pearl of great price, life lived in the Divine One, the search is intensified because what one seeks is "exceedingly precious, beyond all other gains."[7] But as the gospel parable also discloses, "this singular treasure is acquired only at the expense of willingly surrendering every other possession," meaning that "Christ is the pearl of incomparable worth, the fulfillment of spiritual longing."[8]

Mary states further:

> That pearls represent superlative worth is echoed in Jesus' Sermon on the Mount, where he uses the image to warn against careless disregard of holy gifts: *Do not give what is holy to dogs; and do not throw your pearls before swine, or they will trample them underfoot and turn and maul you* (Mt. 7.6). Both Evagrius and Cassian cite this passage in order to remind their readers that "pearls" of spiritual knowledge are not to be given indiscriminately to anyone who

---

[6] See ibid., 60, where the image of a pearl (Christ) is portrayed, around which the chapters on the teaching (VS 22–103) are arranged like spokes of a wheel according to themes, with these in turn encircled by the chs. of Syncletica's early life (VS 4–21) and passion (VS 104–113a), and the final outer layer encompassing the Prologue (VS 1–3) and Epilogue (VS 113b).

[7] Ibid., 40.

[8] Ibid.

is merely curious, but only to people who make a sincere effort to live a holy life. These are ready to discern the voice of wisdom and to accomplish her deeds.[9]

By using the gospel parable of the pearl of great price to open the *Life of Syncletica*, the author points out to hearers and readers of this work that it contains a "thesaurus," that is, a treasure "of spiritual wisdom, of divine knowledge gained by learning the Scriptures with diligent, active faith. But the gift comes with a warning: its wealth will remain hidden to those too negligent to plumb its depths."[10] The author states: "For often pearls of great price go unrecognised by poor men, and those inexperienced in the working of these precious gems scorn them as something small and of no value" (VS 1).

Mary says of a pearl:

[It is] a jewel buried in watery depths, concealed within the very ordinary looking enclosure of an oyster. By virtue of this gem's natural habitat, it is hidden treasure. To discover a pearl one must dive beneath the surface and search for what is not obvious. In a similar way, the *Vita Syncleticae*'s image of a pearl is presented within a thought world where there are levels of knowledge. Even the author admits needing to be trained in order to discern the worth of Syncletica's life and teachings . . . As a result of training . . . , however, the soul is able to discern a beauty in Syncletica's life that engenders supernatural passion and kindles the heart's desire. Rooting out vice and cultivating virtue gradually purifies the heart to contemplate reality with inner eyes. Clarified sight allows the writer to glimpse Christ, the pearl of great price, in the pearl Syncletica. It is this radiant vision that fires the heart with longing. By offering the "pearl of great price" transparent in the amma's *Life* . . . , the author clues the reader that Syncletica aimed at nothing less than union with God. Her search for spiritual wisdom put her on the path of transformation mirroring the transfiguration of Jesus Christ. Syncletica's desire for God refashioned her heart until she

[9] Ibid., 40–41.
[10] Ibid., 41.

> incarnated God's love, pure and simple (VS 22). In Baptism she
> had been clothed in Christ (VS 8, 77). She contemplated his glory,
> putting on his mind and outfitting her life with his deeds.[11]

Thus the whole of Syncletica's teaching is presented as pearls
whose treasure will only be discovered by those who live the truth
of its biblical wisdom in their own lives. Just a few of those pearls
are offered here.

Syncletica opened her discourse on the spiritual life with a
portrayal of the Lord as teacher, "whose breasts supply the milk
of the Old and New Testaments, an image" drawn somewhat from
biblical passages. "While the apostle Paul speaks of providing milk
to the Corinthians who are not yet spiritually mature enough for
solid food (1 Cor 3:2) and while this theme is also taken up in
both Hebrews 5:12-14 and 1 Peter 2:2, the Christian scriptures
make no mention of breast-feeding on the Lord." It is likely that
Syncletica was familiar with the nursing Christ from Clement of
Alexandria's *Paedagogus* I.6, "where the themes of both Christ
nourishing Christians on the breasts of his word and of Christians
drinking the milk of his teaching are mentioned several times."[12]

When disciples come to Syncletica for teaching, her hagiographer indicates that "the blessed woman used to weep, like babes
at the breast" (VS 21). Although Syncletica seemed like an in-
fant, still young enough for breast milk herself, she finally agreed
to teach the other women by presenting morsels she received
from Scripture, that is, "the breasts of the Lord."[13] Her teaching
became like "the pouring [of] the divine draught and water" from
which "each one of the women was receiving what she wanted"
(VS 30). The breast milk of the Scriptures then became "cups of
wisdom" (VS 30) imbibed from the spiritual mother by her spiritual children.

---

[11] Ibid., 41–42.

[12] See Clement of Alexandria, "The Instructor," Ante-Nicene Christian Library
4, trans. William Wilson (Edinburgh: Clark, 1868) 138–39, 143, 144, and 147, as
cited by Forman, "Amma Syncletica," 268.

[13] Forman, "Amma Syncletica," 269.

Modern sensibilities might not relate well to Syncletica's images. However, men and women in her era and world spoke frankly of the human body and had no difficulty in interrelating an everyday image of a breast-feeding mother to the Lord who, like a mother hen, longed to take chicks under his wing (Matt 23:37). But that Syncletica would be seen as providing "cups of wisdom" from biblical teaching incarnated in her own life is uniquely attributed to her as the power of transformation God brings about in her words, as the spirit of the Divine One is conveyed to her disciples.

The images with which she conveys her teaching are often vivid and colorful as she weaves an intricate tapestry of biblical metaphors with scenes drawn from the life around her:

> images of plants and of harvest, . . . of serving at the Master's country estate and at his table; images of building ships and towers, . . . of keeping one's house secure and swept clean; images of learning the alphabet, . . . of carving stone; images of doing laundry and of drawing water, . . . of giving birth and of parenting; images of jewelry and cosmetics and banquets, . . . of armour and battles and war; . . . of treasure hunters and seafarers, . . . of flirts; images of birds and fish and head lice; . . . of dying and decay, images of kindling fire.[14]

Many of these images are ones noticed by a woman living in Alexandria, a port city located on the delta of the Nile River, where women came to wash clothes and observe the people and events around them. For example, in chapter 45, Syncletica states:

> Like a ship our soul is sometimes engulfed by the waves without and is sometimes swamped by the bilge-water within. Certainly we too sometimes perish through sins committed externally, but we sometimes are destroyed by thoughts within us. And so we must guard against onslaughts of spirits from outside us, and bail out impurities of thoughts inside us; and we must always be vigilant with regard to our thoughts, for they are a constant threat to us (VS 45).

[14] Schaffer, *The Life of the Blessed & Holy Syncletica*, Part Two, 43–44.

"Sailors cry out for help" when they are caught in storms, but if they are below deck when "bilge-waters overflow"—which happens "when they are asleep and the sea is calm"—they can easily die (VS 45). She also contrasts those who set out on the ascetical life, who when the sea is calm can easily steer their boats by the light of the "sun of righteousness (Mal 4:2)," that is, Christ, but who, when they are careless and neglect to be vigilant, find they are submerged in dangerous waters, for they forget "the rudder of righteousness" (VS 47); they fail to cry out in the midst of storms to be saved as even worldly people do. Thus speaks a wise woman, who must have experienced failures in vigilance and the dangers of "falling asleep" such that she could describe the reality so clearly to others.

Another favorite image is that of the soul in the midst of temptation, which is likened to a building about to collapse either from the foundation ("good works") or through the roof ("faith") or through its windows ("the senses") (VS 46). One must be quite vigilant against carelessness, "for Scripture says, *Let the one standing firm take care lest he fall* (cf. 1 Cor 10:2)," (VS 46, 48). Falls occur through giving way to the temptations of the vices (VS 49). Those called to live life more intently around the Gospel through the call to virginity (the religious life of her day) must guard against inner attitudes, which can be compared to little insects in a "clean house," quite "visible to all" (VS 80). Again, faults are like poisonous creatures that dwell in "the storerooms of the soul"; for these "we must fumigate our places with the holy incense of prayer . . . with fasting" (VS 80).

Syncletica was fond of teaching that prayer is vital in order to overcome the vice of pride, a particularly problematic passion as one is progressing in the spiritual life. She advises:

> Without ceasing one must meditate upon that inspired word which the blessed David proclaimed when he said: *but I am a worm and not a human being* (Ps 22:6; LXX 21:7). And in another passage Scripture says: *but I am earth and ashes* (Gen 18:27). And also, to be sure, one should listen to that passage of Isaiah, the one which

says: *All human righteousness is like a filthy rag* (cf. Isa 64:6; LXX 64:5; VS 50).

Such verses as remedies against the vices may strike modern ears as harsh and taking some liberties with the texts of Scripture. However, one needs to know the manner in which early Christians read and interpreted biblical texts. For example, the biblical text from Psalm 22:6—"but I am a worm and not a human being"—was often interpreted "spiritually" as an attitude of humility, rather than literally. Posing a contrary remedy for such a vicious attitude as pride was an ancient way to counteract thoughts that, when deeply implanted in the heart, lead to behaviors toward oneself and others that can lead to the ruin of souls. Moreover, considering oneself as a worm and not a human is the attitude attributed to Christ in Psalm 22, several verses of which the evangelist Matthew borrows to show Christ's own humility during his passion.[15] Thus ancient writers, both biblical and monastic, sought to counteract pride with remembrance of the sufferings of Christ, who was completely reduced in his humanity. This counter-remedy is a call to go to the Scriptures and to find there the exemplar of what it means to be human, the one who took upon himself all our sins. The phrase, "I am earth and ashes" from Genesis 18:27 again serves to remind its hearers that, no matter how much they exalt human accomplishment, they all die and return to the earth. Every Ash Wednesday Christians hear these words, "Remember that you are dust and unto dust you shall return." The last biblical phrase, taken from Isaiah 64:6, reminds Christians that no amount of righteousness by human measuring wins God's favor; thus, "all human righteousness (good deeds) is like a filthy rag." None of these sayings has anything to do with modern preoccupations with self-esteem. The biblical phrases are theological truths, reminding arrogant-prone human

[15] See, for example, the citation of Ps 22:8 in Matt 27:39-40; Ps 22:9 in Matt 27:43; and Ps 22:2a in Matt 27:46. Benedict, in his sixth century Rule, cites Ps 22:6 in his seventh step of humility (*Rule of Benedict* 7.52) in keeping with the spiritual interpretation of the early Church.

beings that God is God and humans are not God. Anyone struggling with being their own god is to heed the prophetic words of Scripture, lest they fall.

As Mary Schaffer has noted of Syncletica,

> It is readily apparent that the *Vita Syncleticae* is steeped in biblical references and allusions. Syncletica supplies a Scripture verse for nearly every situation she describes in the ascent to holiness. Scripture may offer authoritative counsel, bolstering a point the amma is making. Scripture may enhance what she is saying by suggesting a symbolic or spiritual meaning beyond her obvious, practical advice. Syncletica may invoke a Scripture passage more than once, thereby connecting teachings and providing a richer meditation on the text. At the same time, the repetition suggests that this passage recurs in Syncletica's own prayer, offering her sustenance again and again (VS 10, 57, 93, 99, 111). Spurred by the joy she knows is waiting if only they persist (VS 60), the amma urges her listeners to let nothing impede prayer: not illness (VS 99; AS 8), not useless grief, distraction or despair (VS 86, 42-43, 40; AS 27), not trials or temptation or the increase of them, for one must always lean on the gracious mercy of God (VS 98; AS 7). Thus, Syncletica prays without ceasing. Her converse with God is the life-long, intimate dialogue of a sturdy relationship, covenanted in love (VS 60, 92, 9). She hears St. Paul's admonition to pray without ceasing (1 Thes. 5.17), not as a challenge to her schedule, but as an invitation to offer her Saviour her whole mind and so become a "custodian of pure love" (VS 43, 71). The purity of one's prayer and the purity of one's actions are in direct relationship. Genuine charity testifies to pure prayer because deeds of love rise from contemplation. But the reverse is also true. Contempt for others corrupts prayer, destroys the capacity for love and generates hatred toward others. . . . Prayer requires that body and soul together shape an attitude of humility and praise regardless of external circumstances or interior dispositions, thereby honoring the true and fundamental relationship between creature and Creator, between Beloved and loved.[16]

---

[16] Schaffer, *The Life of the Blessed & Holy Syncletica*, Part Two, 89–90. "AS" in the parentheses refers to the number of the apophthegm attributed to Syncletica

CONTEMPORARY EXAMPLE

When I reflect on an *amma* in my own community who, like Syncletica, loved pearls of wisdom, I think of Sister Theresa. When I made my final profession in 1982, Sister Theresa was going on her one-hundredth year of life and seventy-fifth jubilee. When she was ninety-one, she and I became acquainted. As soon as I would come home from summer school, she would meet at the door and she would say, "Sister Mary, you must come to my room and tell me what you learned." I would go to her room and tell her what I learned. One day, while I was working in the infirmary getting the meds put together (also it was my turn for night duty in the infirmary, and I was preparing a class for the novices), Sister Theresa came in and sat in the rocking chair and asked, "Sister Mary, what are you reading?" I answered, "I am reading Karl Rahner who is describing how Jesus has this intimate, contemplative awareness of God, his father." She said, "Read it to me." I said, "Yes, Sister." So I read the passage to her, which was about two pages long. You know, I've never been able to find those two pages again. After I was done, she looked at me and said, "Again." So I started over and read the whole passage a second time. Then she looked at me and said, "One more time." "All right, Sister," I said a little puzzled, and so I read it one more time. She was teaching me how to do *lectio*. After I read it the third time, she smiled and said, "Karl Rahner is right, you know." Then she got up and trotted off down the hall to her room!

I did not know until a few years ago that she read Karl Rahner in the original German, and she was a first-grade teacher until she retired at age eighty-five.

---

in the work, *The Sayings of the Desert Fathers: The Alphabetical Collection*, Cistercian Studies 59, trans. Benedicta Ward (London & Oxford: Mowbray/U.S.A.: Cistercian Publications, 1975); see pp. 230–35 of this edition.

REFLECTION EXERCISE

I invite you to spend time with the Matthean parable of the pearl (Matt 13:44-46) and ask the Lord to reveal to you how precious you are to him, and to bring to you a deepening desire for how precious the Lord is to you. You may wish to explore your relationship and the signposts of coming to cherish each other and what a treasure the relationship has been for you. For example, you might revisit significant moments of your faith life such as your learning about the Creator, your childhood understanding of Jesus and the Holy Spirit, and how that knowledge shifted as you entered adolescence and adulthood. Think about how your knowledge of God changed again as you entered a community or significant relationship. It is important that you call on the Holy Spirit to remind you of these moments and what they have meant from the Holy One's perspective. After you review together, then ask the Lord to show you where you are being called to grow— that is, where the cherishing between you can deepen, and what pearls are being held out to you today.

FURTHER SCRIPTURAL PASSAGES FOR PRAYER

Matthew 7:6-11	Pearls before swine and answer to prayer
Luke 12:32-34	Treasure in heaven
1 Corinthians 3:1-9	Spiritual food
Hebrews 5:11-14	Spiritual food
1 Peter 2:2-10	Spiritual food
Psalm 22	Prayer of the Innocent Suffering Person
Genesis 18:27 in 18:22-33	Abraham's bartering with God over the innocent
Isaiah 64:1-11	God's attitude about unrighteousness

6 Humility and the Manifestation of Thoughts

OPENING REFLECTION: Psalm 32

Lord God, you call us blessed when we acknowledge our sinfulness and failings to you. We praise and thank you for the blessing of your forgiving love in Jesus Christ and your reconciling presence in your Holy Spirit. We rejoice in your sheltering presence and in your nearness even when we distress you. Grant us the grace necessary to walk in the way you mark out for us and the receptive heart needed to heed your words. We ask all this in the name of the One in whom our sins are covered over, Jesus Christ, our Lord. Amen.

INTRODUCTORY REMARKS

The topic of humility and manifestation of thoughts was a very important part of the spiritual direction that took place between an *amma* or *abba* and the disciple, who chose and came to the wise elder seeking a word of life. For several days now I've mentioned the thoughts, and it is time to explain what the ancient tradition meant by the term *thoughts*, or *logismoi* (in Greek) for the plural or *logismos* (singular, thought).

In the ancient Eastern monastic tradition, the manifestation of thoughts *(logismoi)* was considered a process of transformation. The *logismoi* are not the fleeting thoughts of our mind to which most of the time we hardly pay attention, things like, "I'm so tired today. I've got all these things to do after prayer. I'd rather be taking a nap." Rather, *logismoi* are those thoughts that the ancients called demonic, passionate, or derived from self-will, that is, the will that stands in opposition to God's loving designs and desires for us. A *logismos* arises as an attractive image stirring the mind; it is a passionate movement that incites the person to a secret decision against God's law or can present "itself as some sort of idol." It can be a seeming good, like holding up a practice, ideal, or pursuit, which becomes more important than God. This is how Evagrius, the Greek systematician of the desert spiritual life, described these kinds of evil thoughts.[1] Other Eastern spiritual writers spoke of "the degrees of penetration" of these evil thoughts into the heart, from the moment of the appearance of temptation to the decision in the will: to act against God or another. The first stage is the *suggestion* or the "simple idea or image suggested to the mind or the heart by 'the enemy.'" The second stage is "the *drawing near,* the *coupling,* which is 'parleying' with the suggested object (to do it or not?)." The next stage is the *"mental consent* to some forbidden pleasure," which can become sin. Consent moves to "the *inner struggle,"* which becomes "decisive for consent." The final stage is called *"captivity,"* whereby the heart is carried away by the passion, which becomes "a vicious habit" as a result of a long series of assents.[2] These thoughts are mulled and brooded over until they take root like weeds in the soil of one's heart and eventually manifest themselves as uncharitable behaviors of all kinds.

A long line of early monastic men and women were concerned about such thoughts and their manifestations because, often, the directee was unable to distinguish between helpful and harmful thoughts or even ones that are indifferent. The spiritual elder was concerned with rooting these thoughts out; through the grace of

---

[1] Tomáš Špidlik, *The Spirituality of the Christian East,* Cistercian Studies 79, trans. Anthony P. Gythiel (Kalamazoo: Cistercian Publications, 1986) 238–39.

[2] Ibid., 238–40. The words in *italics* show my emphasis.

God's Spirit, all the thoughts, fantasies, fancies, revolts, vices, ideas, and movements of the heart were presented in conversation so that there could be a distinguishing of the thoughts of God from thoughts coming from elsewhere. The one manifesting his/her thoughts was invited in the process to put on the mindfulness of Christ by clothing oneself in the humility of self-disclosure.

Although the elder was expected to be trustworthy, discerning, an inspired and trusted companion to the disciple manifesting his/her thoughts, the disciple's role was also important. While the spiritual elder was "witness and encourager," s/he did not control the process. The whole point of confession of faults and manifestation of thoughts—good, bad, and indifferent (this practice is not to be confused with confession of sin)—was the opening up of the self to God as a means of committing oneself to the truth and as a predisposition to contemplating God. Another way of saying this is that the monastic person undertook "the ascetical labor of self-knowledge": "to see things as they are, and to see God as God can be seen, without masks of fantasy, projections, pious wishes," by stripping away "the masks of fantasies and projections about ourselves."[3]

Today one would say that if s/he is troubled by the behavior of another, s/he is being invited to look at her/his own behavior. Another person can serve as a mirror of one's own self. Maybe one needs to take back one's projections and see what it is in oneself that needs healing and enlightenment. "The goal of the desert was utter transparence to divine light. The elder, far from being a center of power and a 'director', served in his or her transparence to divine light as a lens which could focus the light of truth on the dark places in the disciple's heart."[4] In desert spirituality the point was the development of humility and obedience, rather than penitence and pardon.

---

[3] Columba Stewart, "The Desert Fathers on Radical Self-Honesty," *Vox Benedictina* 8.1 (Summer 1991) 10–11.

[4] Ibid., 11.

STORIES AND COMMENTARY

Amma Theodora was famous for teaching that humility is key to driving out demonic thoughts when she said the following: "[N]either asceticism nor vigils nor any kind of suffering are able to save, only true humility can do that. There was an anchorite who was able to banish the demons; and he asked them, 'What makes you go away? Is it fasting?' They replied, 'We do not eat or drink?' 'Is it vigils?' They replied, 'We do not sleep.' 'Is it separation from the world?' 'We live in the deserts.' 'What power sends you away then?' They said, 'Nothing can overcome us, but only humility.' 'Do you see how humility is victorious over the demons?'"[5]

It may well be that Theodora was this monk's mentor, which could be the reason why she knew the story so well. She does not actually tell us that, but obviously she believed the wisdom of the humility learned by the monk who was graced with this gift, otherwise she would not have repeated it. It was an important piece of monastic wisdom and so it was remembered and ultimately written down.

As one grows deeper in the faith journey, one comes face-to-face with the reality of sin—the ways one gives into temptation, the subtleties of one's own devious thoughts, the darkness that lurks below the surface of this sweet-appearing person. All this must be yielded up to Christ in the person of the trusted elder.

What is fascinating is that, at least in some circles of psychology, this issue of sin and temptation is surfacing. Dr. M. Scott Peck, a number of years ago in his book, *The Road Less Traveled*, said that the story of Adam and Eve's fall only began to make sense in his life as he wrestled with the question of why some patients got well in psychotherapy, while others did not. Part of the answer for him came through the insight into his own laziness and that of many humans. What he found was missing in the

---

[5] "Theodora #6," in *The Sayings of the Desert Fathers: The Alphabetical Collection*, Cistercian Studies 59, trans. Benedicta Ward (London & Oxford: Mowbray/U.S.A.: Cistercian Publications, 1975) 84.

Fall story of Genesis is any recognition by Adam and Eve to get "God's side of the issue"; they refused to ask or challenge God as adults as to why they were not to eat the fruit of good and evil, and took the path of least resistance by believing and blaming the serpent. Their fall was a failure "to consult or listen to God within them, the knowledge of rightness," which is inherent in human nature.[6] If they had done the hard work of listening to God, which requires time, energy, and humility, they would have discovered themselves being urged on the more difficult pathway—the path of greater effort to resist their evil suggestions. To have opened themselves to wrestling with God in dialogue and debate would have meant opening themselves "to suffering and struggle."[7]

The basis of much laziness, which Peck addresses, is fear—fear of change, fear of facing how humans rationalize comfortable forms of relating with each other, fear of loss that if one begins to grow, change, and live by more constructive and healthy patterns, this will shift one's friendships, the ways one is pictured in one's community or family, how one relates with others. And it certainly will. Then there is the other fear—that of accepting responsibility for one's life and decisions by choosing not to blame one's history, family, community, or situation in the world. The way to health, says Dr. Peck, is the way through the reality of sin as it manifests itself sometimes in symptoms of some forms of mental illness, in lack of awareness, and/or resistance to the demands of conversion.[8]

The monastic way to health, to holiness and wholeness, is by humbly opening oneself to the human condition, with its sinful thoughts tempting one's heart, by refusing to conceal the secret wrongs one has done, and by confession to a spiritual friend. The monastic heritage emphasizes this as the beginning of healing, as was seen in the case of Evagrius manifesting his broken promise to

---

[6] M. Scott Peck, M.D., *The Road Less Traveled* (New York: A Touchstone Book, Simon and Schuster, 1978) 273.

[7] Ibid.

[8] Ibid., 275–76, 291.

God before Amma Melania. Another example is one taken from the stories associated with Abba Lot:

> It was related of a brother who had committed a fault that when he went to Abba Lot, he was troubled and hesitated, going in and coming out, unable to sit down. Abba Lot said to him, "What is the matter, brother?" He said, "I have committed a great fault and I cannot acknowledge it to the Fathers." The old man said to him, "Confess it to me, and I will carry it." Then he said to him, "I have fallen into fornication, and in order to do it, I have sacrificed to idols." The old man said to him, "Have confidence; repentance is possible. Go, sit in your cave, eat only once in two days and I will carry half of your fault with you." After three weeks, the old man had the certainty that God had accepted the brother's repentance. Then the latter remained in submission to the old man until his death.[9]

There are at least two significant moments in the story. The first is the disciple's willingness to confess himself to Abba Lot. The second is the *abba's* loving willingness to carry half the fault, or rather the repentance for the fault, with the brother monk who was suffering and, in turn, give the brother a word of hope: "Have confidence; repentance is possible." Note that the brother had to bear his share and not place the whole load on his elder. In the sharing of the penance and prayer and fasting with the brother, Abba Lot received the word from God that God had forgiven the brother and Abba Lot, in turn, passed that word along to the brother.

What would happen in communities and families if they trusted one another with the need for support through a loathsome temptation, and the one in whom the care was confided was willing to carry the burden in discretion and confidentiality by fasting and praying for the one in need? What if communities fasted and prayed for the abused children, battered wives, and broken husbands, siblings, and relatives we know? What chan-

---

[9] "Lot #2," in *The Sayings of the Desert Fathers*, 122.

nels of God's grace might our faith communities become for our world!

According to Cassian, a favorite author whom Syncletica likely read, "One teaches beginners not to hide by false shame any of the thoughts which consume their heart, but, as soon as they appear, to manifest them to the elder, and, in order to pass judgment on them, not to trust in one's own personal opinion, but to believe evil or good that which the elder, after examination, will declare to be such. . . . The elders affirm, in effect, that it is a universal and evident sign of a diabolical thought if we hesitate to manifest it to the elder."[10]

Cassian attributes a liberating effect to the admission of faults, especially secret faults and burdensome spiritual problems. The will to express is a sign of "discretion." The ability for candid, trusting speech (*parrhesia* in Greek) is a gift of the Spirit—both for the one manifesting her/himself and for the spiritual midwife.[11] Biblical *parrhesia* or trusting speech "can be interpreted as the gift of being able to open oneself in confidence to the Lord and to the Lord's agents."[12]

This confession of self is not the same as psychotherapy nor was it necessarily related to the understanding of the sacrament of reconciliation. Nor should this act of humility be in any way equated with forced manifestation of thoughts, as a young sister related concerning her newly founded community. There the priest-founder called for private manifestation of conscience every week by the sisters to him alone. This kind of action on his part is a gross violation of choice of spiritual mentor on the part of the directee, as well as a violation of conscience. Whenever the desire to control or have power over others is a motive for seemingly

---

[10] As cited by Emmanuel Latteur, "Les douze degres d'humilité de la Règle de saint Benoît restent-ils actuels?" *Collectanea Cisterciensia* 45 (1983) 253–54.

[11] Georg Holzherr, *Die Benediktsregel: Eine Anleitung zu Christlichem Leben*, trans. Terrence Kardong, 91, in a private English translation.

[12] Terrence Kardong, *Benedict's Rule: A Commentary* (Collegeville: Liturgical Press, 1995) 152.

good observances, one must beware. The Spirit of God operates in freedom from control, anxiety, fear, and coercion.

For many moderns the psychoanalyst or confessor has replaced the role of the spiritual *amma* or *abba*. Primarily the role of the latter was one of listener to the heart of another in order to help them discern the motivations, drives, and impulses of their lives. It took an act of faith to believe that the revelation of the self would bring the power of Christ's transforming-transfiguring love, as mediated through a holy person, who had already been journeying some time on this path of holiness. This elder had experienced the discerning judgment and consoling mercy of God and out of her/his silence, a healing word or gesture of love would bring the hope of forgiveness and healing.

CONTEMPORARY EXAMPLE

One summer as a college student I lived in Appalachia, wanting to learn more about poverty in rural America. At the close of my summer in the "hollers" of southern Pennsylvania, I met Mrs. Gulanik, a Czechoslovakian refugee, who had seen her teenage son shot at the door of her house by the communists, because he had dared to continue attending church with his mother. When I asked her what she missed most about her life in Czechoslovakia, she said, "In America, everyone is friendly, but I have no friend to share my heart with. In my village the *babunia* heard all our sorrows and heartaches and faults and prayed and cried with us and somehow we knew God's love." Mrs. Gulanik was expressing a universal human need for a *babunia*—an *amma*, someone wise in the ways of God and of the human heart, one who could receive the pain, suffering, and perhaps even the effects of the sin of those around her and carry the burden of infirmity, in confidentiality and loving mercy, so that the members of the community might know God's love in their midst.

REFLECTION EXERCISE

If you choose, I invite you to spend some time reflecting on a time in your life when you were aware of your own frailty, capacity for temptation, even sin. Ask the Lord to be with you in this reflection and to reveal to you how much you were being loved, even in the midst of this time of seeming absence of God's love. Listen attentively to his Spirit as you are guided through this reflection so you may know God's mercy. What expression of gratitude might you offer?

FURTHER SCRIPTURAL PASSAGES FOR PRAYER

Psalm 32   Candid admission of sin
Psalm 118   Processional hymn to God's love
Psalm 37   The fate of the virtuous and the wicked
Psalm 106   National confession
Isaiah 38:16-20   Canticle on the faithful, healing love of God

7

Penthos and Tears—
Signs of Conversion

OPENING REFLECTION: Matthew 5: 1-12—The Beatitudes

Of all these beatitudes, which Jesus recommended were to be the attitudes of disciples, the second, "Blest too the sorrowing, for they shall be consoled," was the one most highly prized by the early desert ascetics. This attitude of penthos or sorrow most frequently manifested itself in the gift of tears, also highly prized in early monasticism.

So we pray: O God, you who always hear the cries of the poor and long to wipe away every tear from our eyes, teach us the wisdom of compunction of heart, that we may long to see with your eyes of compassion, kindness, mercy and justice on the world you made to manifest your presence. However we may have experienced sorrow, let us see it from your perspective, which is so much deeper, wider and broader than our own way of seeing. We ask this in the name of compassion, Jesus Christ, our Lord. Amen.

INTRODUCTORY REMARKS

Compunction, the attitude that comes from the grace-filled self-knowledge that one is a sinner in need of redemption, translates two Greek words: *penthos*, or sorrow, and *katanyxis*, which is "a sudden shock, an emotion which plants deep in the soul a feeling, an attitude, or a resolution."[1] The way the early tradition understood the connection between *katanyxis* and *penthos* was that the monk or nun became aware through some kind of external experience that he or she had committed a fault, been negligent, or was not vigilant and so had succumbed to temptation. The awareness struck him or her powerfully so that the compunction led to a concomitant sorrow, which in turn continued on into the gift of tears, for each knew that there are always consequences to one's negligence, omission or outright commission of a fault. Tears often began as an expression of sorrow for the offense against God and/or another, but then the tears were often transformed into joy over the benevolent, generous mercy of God.

"Amma Syncletica said, 'In the beginning there are a great many battles and a good deal of suffering for those who are advancing towards God and afterwards, ineffable joy. It is like those who wish to light a fire; at first they are choked by the smoke and cry, and by this means obtain what they seek (as it is said: "Our God is a consuming fire" [Heb. 12.24]): so we also must kindle the divine fire in ourselves through tears and hard work.'"[2] Amma Syncletica and other wise elders knew the value of these tears for preparing the soil of the heart, to soften it to receive God's graces.

There is an awareness in the early monastic tradition of a "godly sorrow," that is, a way one lived in consciousness of being a person in need of repentance and also of being thankful at the same time. For example, Mark the Hermit taught that *"penthos* without thanksgiving would be despair, sorrow that was not godly, while thanksgiving without repentance would be a presumptuous illusion."[3] There is such a fine line in the spiritual life between an

---

[1] Irénée Hausherr, *Penthos: The Doctrine of Compunction in the Christian East*, Cistercian Studies 53, trans. Anselm Hufstader (Kalamazoo: Cistercian Publications, 1982) 8.

[2] "Syncletica #1," in *The Sayings of the Desert Fathers: The Alphabetical Collection*, Cistercian Studies 59, trans. Benedicta Ward (London & Oxford: Mowbray/U.S.A.: Cistercian Publications, 1975) 230–31.

[3] Hausherr, *Penthos*, 19.

awareness of how much we stand in need of God's mercy without slipping into hopelessness, and at the same time of being deeply grateful for the gifts God has bestowed on us without taking the entire credit on ourselves.

STORIES AND COMMENTARY

One of the most powerful stories of repentance is that of Maria, the niece of the anchorite Abraham, which is told in *Harlots of the Desert*.[4] Briefly, the story relates that when the brother of Abba Abraham died, he left his only daughter, a seven-year-old named Maria. Friends brought the child to Abraham, knowing no other relative to whom to entrust her. So Abraham arranged that a small room be added onto his cell for her, with a window in the wall between their two cells through which he spoke to her, teaching her the Psalter and other Scriptures, the manner of keeping vigils and singing the praises of the Lord. The little girl imitated her uncle in his ascetical practices. As she grew in holiness, Abraham prayed with tears that she would be spared the snares of the Devil and the traps of evil thoughts. Thus they lived together in peace and harmony for twenty years.[5]

Now there was a young man, a monk in name only, who came to visit Abraham and soon increased the frequency of his visits out of a desire to speak to Maria through the window. One day he came to her outside cell window and persuaded her to climb down to him. He lay with her and then left. She was appalled at what she had done, and was overcome with great grief and anxiety, saying to herself: "I feel as if I am dead already; I have lost all that I had before by the hard work of asceticism; all my prayers, tears and vigils have come to nothing. I have angered God and destroyed myself. Alas, I am utterly miserable. I ought to become a

---

[4] Benedicta Ward, *Harlots of the Desert: A Study of Repentance in Early Monastic Sources* (London & Oxford: Mowbray, 1987). The English translation of "Maria the Niece of Abraham" is found on pages 92–101.

[5] "Maria the Niece of Abraham," in *Harlots*, 92–93.

fountain all made of tears. I have brought down sorrow upon my most holy uncle. The shame, o my soul, overwhelms me. I have been mocked by the devil. What is there for me but wretchedness if I live any longer . . . "[6] [and so on for many more verses].

This kind of grieving is not the healthy kind of compunction and sorrow noted at the beginning of the chapter, but an unhealthy sorrow that *ammas* and *abbas* alike were quick to discourage in their disciples because it led to a self-preoccupation with the loss of achievement of the ascetical process by one's own efforts alone. Even worse, it led to despair of God's mercy, toward which healthy sorrow always leads.

The upshot of this way of thinking, which was a source of temptation, was that Maria thought that there was no chance now for her salvation; so she went to a nearby city, changed her appearance, and plied her trade as a prostitute. But then Abraham received a dream in which he saw a serpent entering Maria's cell and snatched a dove. When he prayed to know the meaning of the dream, two days later he saw a snake come into his own cell and place its head under Abraham's feet and die, but the dove, still alive, came out of the serpent's stomach. When Abraham called to Maria in her cell, he received no reply.[7] For two years he prayed constantly for her, not knowing where she was. One day he received word from a friend who had made inquiries about her whereabouts. Abraham immediately asked for soldier's clothing and a horse so that he might journey in disguise to find his niece.[8] Disguise is a favorite hagiographical theme, for it "functions to show Abraham as one who imitates Christ who came hidden in the flesh."[9]

---

[6] Ibid., 93–94.

[7] Ibid., 94.

[8] Ibid., 95.

[9] Lynne W. Smith, paper entitled "Sanctity in *Life of Maria the Harlot* and *The Fall and Repentance of Mary*," prepared for Monastic Studies class, "Monastic Sanctity: Saints and Sinners through the Ages" (St. John's University, School of Theology, May 9, 2001) 5.

When Abraham arrived at the brothel, the brothel keeper was only too happy to turn Maria over to this old man. When Abraham approached Maria to kiss her, she smelled the odor of asceticism on him and was puzzled by this old man whom she did not recognize. However, she burst into tears at that point because she remembered her days with her uncle and noticed a certain resemblance in the old man.[10] Once Abraham had paid the brothel keeper the required money and had entered Maria's inner chamber, he took off the hat he had been wearing,[11] and with a tearful voice spoke to Maria, saying, "Don't you know me, Maria my child? Dear heart, am I not he who took care of you? What happened, my dear? Who hurt you, my daughter? . . . Why, when you sinned, did you not tell me? Why could you not come and speak of it with me? For of course I would have done penance for you. I and our dearest Ephraim. [Ephraim was a fellow desert father and close friend to both Abraham and Maria, as well as narrator of the story.] . . . For who is without sin, save God alone?"[12]

Maria, for her part, sat like a stone and refused to speak so that Abraham might continue speaking to her of God's loving forgiveness, and covering her with his tears. Finally, in the middle of the night, she burst into tears and replied: "I could not come to you; I was so very much ashamed. How can I pray again to God when I am defiled with sin which is as filthy as this?"[13] Abraham tried to persuade her to let him carry her sin and for her to come back home with him. Even Ephraim was grieving and praying for her return. Then Abraham shared the most important advice of all:

> My dear, do not draw back from the mercy of God. To you, your sins seem like mountains, but God has spread his mercy over all that He has made. So we once read together how an unclean woman came to the Lord and he did not send her away but cleansed her,

[10] Ward, "Maria the Niece of Abraham," 96.
[11] Ibid., 97.
[12] Ibid., 98.
[13] Ibid.

and she washed his feet with her tears and wiped them with the hairs of her head. If sparks could set fire to the ocean, then indeed your sins could defile the purity of God! It is not new to fall, my daughter; what is wrong is to lie down when you have fallen. Remember where you stood before you fell. The Devil once mocked you, but now he will know that you can rise more strong than ever before. I beg you, take pity on my old age and do not make me grieve any more. Get up and come with me to our cell. Do not be afraid; sin is only part of being human; it happened to you very quickly and now by the help of God you are coming out of it even more quickly, for he does not will the death of sinners, but rather that they may live.[14]

What is so powerful about this encounter is the deep love with which Abraham conveys the message of God's forgiving love and the wisdom of relying on that mercy, rather than concentrating on the sin. Moreover, God knows that human beings sin and God does not will the death of the sinner; rather, God's deepest desire is that the sinner know and experience God's mercy. Abraham takes the part of the Lord in the latter's encounter with the woman who repented.

On hearing words like this, Maria placed her head on Abraham's feet and wept away the rest of the night. In the morning she was persuaded to accompany Abraham back to their cells. He is described by Ephraim as follows: "He placed her on the horse and he went first leading it, like a shepherd with the lost sheep he had found, bearing it home upon his shoulders with joy. So with a glad heart Abraham made the journey home with his niece."[15] One cannot help but hear an echo of Luke's parable of divine mercy, about the shepherd going after the lost sheep and then returning home with it with great joy that he has found it, even to the extent of hosting a party with his friends, from Luke 15:1-7. This parable was a favorite of many early monastic and early Christian writers, for no pastor of souls could contemplate being anything

[14] Ibid., 98–99.
[15] Ibid., 99.

other than Christ, the shepherd to any lost soul. So stories like the one told of Abraham and Maria served as reminders to elders of their loving obligation to imitate the Lord when they had the opportunity.

Ephraim further tells us that Maria undertook a rigorous repentance, lamenting her sins with tears and lamentation loud enough to be heard by passersby. She asked God for a sign that she had been forgiven and, after three years, was graced with the gift of healing. "Crowds of people came to her daily and she would heal them all by her prayers for their salvation," states Ephraim.[16] Abraham lived another ten years after these events and died in his seventieth year, having lived for fifty years as a hermit "with great endurance, humility of heart and love unfeigned."[17] Maria lived another five years after her uncle's death, continuing to weep and pray to the Lord.[18]

This story of Abraham and Maria illustrates the three kinds of sorrow that Amma Syncletica taught. "There is grief that is useful, and there is grief that is destructive. The first sort consists in weeping over one's own faults and weeping over the weakness of one's neighbours, in order not to destroy one's purpose, and attach oneself to the perfect good. But there is also a grief that comes from the enemy, full of mockery, which some call *accidie*. This spirit must be cast out, mainly by prayer and psalmody."[19]

When Maria had sinned and realized it, she was pierced to the heart, but she gave way to the temptation of despairing of God's mercy, which, in turn, led her to forsake her vocation and turn to prostitution. Such despair represents an ungodly, destructive sorrow. When Abraham learns that Maria is gone, he weeps on her behalf, as also does Ephraim, Abraham's disciple and friend; their sorrow is a weeping over the weakness of their beloved "daughter." Their prayers and tears are answered by God, who visits

[16] Ibid.
[17] Ibid., 99–100.
[18] Ibid., 100.
[19] "Syncletica #27," in *Sayings of the Desert Fathers*, 235.

Abraham with news of Maria's whereabouts and sets the desire in Abraham's heart to go and find her. When he does find her and asks her why she left him, he again weeps tears of the healthy sort out of a deep love for her and desire for her to know God's tender mercy. It is when she experiences this mercy in the human flesh of Abraham's pleading and tears that Maria receives a gift of tears that is healthy. In other words, her tears of bitterness and despair are transformed by the Christ-like love of her uncle into tears of repentance. After three years of heartfelt penitence, her tears become those of joy, manifested in healing gifts on behalf of many who come to her. Her tears have made a place of divine presence in her life so that she is as Christ to all who come for healing and compassion. She, who was wounded by the darts of the evil one and healed by the love of Christ-made-flesh in her uncle, becomes the presence of Christ transfigured to others. That is what is meant by the wisdom of tears as a means of salvation.

CONTEMPORARY EXAMPLE

A few years ago I was pierced to the heart by the words a colleague said to me. As I pondered those words, it occurred to me that I was placing far more importance on what this person thought of me than probably was necessary. I did not know how to get out of that pit. One day when I was at prayer, I asked God to deliver me from this unhealthy sorrow. As I sat in prayer, one of the things that came to me (and only in the wisdom of the Spirit do these things happen) was the memory of the death of my father when I was seventeen years old. He had been diagnosed with leukemia when I was fourteen, and he actually lived two and one-half years longer than the doctors anticipated. One thing he lived for was to see his oldest daughter Mary graduate from high school. I have a memory of my dad wanting to take a picture of me before graduation and my refusing that request. So Dad went up into the bleachers and I sat with the rest of my graduating class. Then I walked across the stage and picked up my diploma. My dad clapped and then collapsed in the bleachers. My mom had to ask two men beside them to carry my dad to the car, and she took him to the hospital for the last time. He died a week later.

What I had not realized until the Spirit brought the awareness back to me is how much my refusing my dad had left the impression that I discounted his love in some way. So I had been on a search for many years for the approval of certain men in my life, especially those who might resemble my father. I did not even know this. In the prayer that day, I saw my father's face and I experienced the tremendous love my father had for this daughter, that he lived long enough to see her get her diploma. I finally realized, with tears streaming down my face, that Christ was visiting me in my father's love, and it transformed the interpretation of that experience that I had carried for almost forty years in my heart. It also transformed my need to be approved of in certain kinds of ways and to trust that God would be the one who would heal me, love me, and sustain me.

What I know from that experience of prayer as I have reflected upon it since is that that kind of visitation of the Holy Spirit is always a gift. God always knows when our heart is ready to deal with a sorrow in our lives in a new way, in a deeper way. When our spirit cries out to God's Spirit, God's Spirit, who hears that need, will bring what we need to heal it.

REFLECTION EXERCISE

I invite you in your prayer today to reflect on the gift of compunction in your own life. You may wish to consider where the Lord has led you through a time of struggle with temptation or a fault or sin, maybe a past experience, where you need to re-experience the tenderness of divine mercy and forgiveness. Or you may wish to remember a time when your own heart was pierced with compunction and compassion for another, someone caught in a tough situation and needed you to reach out to her/him with God's merciful understanding and goodness. Ask the Spirit to guide your meditation on either of these situations and, if the Spirit wishes you to know, reveal the fruit of these encounters.

FURTHER SCRIPTURAL PASSAGES FOR PRAYER

Psalm 51	The Miserere: prayer of repentance
Psalm 126	Sowing in tears
Isaiah 61:1-3	Mission to the afflicted
Luke 15:1-7,	
8-10, 11-32	Three parables of divine mercy
Revelations 21:1-7	New heavens

8

The Hidden Life

OPENING REFLECTION: Matthew 6:1-4—
"On the Purity of Intention"

O God of hiddenness and of the anawim, it is not easy for us to be unobtrusive and unassuming, as manifestations of your inner glory within us. This day teach us the meaning of living that draws attention to your goodness and grace, rather than our own pursuit of a reputation built solely on what others think of us. In whatever ways we need to grow in a self-love that is a reflection of your own loving of us, send us your grace to be fully the images and likenesses of your presence. We trust that you will answer us as we pray in the name of Jesus Christ, our Lord. Amen.

INTRODUCTORY REMARKS

The theme of this chapter, "The Hidden Life," is not one that is readily understood in Western culture. Part of the reason for that is that westerners live in post-Enlightenment and post-Freudian times, meaning that rationalism, psychology, and self-fulfillment are so much a part of our human self-understanding that these values color what is read and heard from earlier cultures. Consequently, modern readers find themselves repulsed by those who appear to lack in "self-esteem." At times it is necessary to look at how this psychological reading of ancient texts, like the Bible and early monastic writings, does a disservice to the profound theological and religious truths that are being conveyed. One need not disparage psychology, for it does a great service to people, but it just does not go far enough into understanding the human person, especially as understood in early monastic spirituality.

So, for example, in the reading from Matthew with which the chapter opened, the evangelist is warning his audience about the show of religious works. The context of the words, "Be on guard against performing religious acts for people to see. . . . Keep your deeds of mercy secret, and your Father who sees in secret will re-pay you" (Matt 6:1, 4), is not at all a matter of not being proud in the good sense of being religious people. Rather the gospel context is one in which hypocrites are the focus. *Hypocrites* is Greek for "actors," those folks who were on stage in ancient cultures and who wore masks behind which they performed their plays; some-one had to blow the horn to get the audience's attention that the play was about to begin.[1] The reward for a good performance was applause, which the hypocrites sought above all else, for applause signaled approval, perhaps payment for the performance, as well as indicating the future potential for many more opportunities to act. While acting was held in high regard in the Greco-Roman cul-ture, it was not held in esteem by the Jews nor by early Christians because of the many other ways actors had to earn money to feed themselves, often selling their bodies for coins.[2]

Given this background on the acting profession, it is little won-der that Matthew contrasts the motivation of the hypocrite with that of the disciple. A disciple is most deeply concerned with pleasing God, who sees all that the disciple does and rewards, not in empty applause, but with the grace of provident care. Also, Matthew is concerned about the condition of the heart, from which flows the fruit of one's motivations:

---

[1] Daniel J. Harrington, "Matthew," in *The Collegeville Bible Commentary*, ed. Dianne Bergant and Robert J. Karris (Collegeville: Liturgical Press, 1989) 872.

[2] Benedicta Ward, *Harlots of the Desert: A Study of Repentance in Early Mo-nastic Sources* (London & Oxford: Mowbray, 1987) 104.

> Do not lay up for yourselves an earthly treasure. Moths and rust
> corrode; thieves break in and steal. Make it your practice instead
> to store up heavenly treasure, which neither moths nor rust cor-
> rode nor thieves break in and steal. Remember, where your trea-
> sure is, there your heart is also (Matt 6:19-21).[3]

So it is the intentionality of the heart, where the treasuring oc-
curs, that preoccupies ancient Christian writers and calls them to
portray stories of hidden sanctity in the ways that they do.

In Eastern spirituality the heart is the center of all religion
and of all mysticism, as "the foundation of the Christian life."[4]
According to Tomáš Špidlík, scholar of Eastern spirituality, Eastern writers "speak of custody of the heart, of attentiveness to the
heart, of purity of the heart, of the thoughts, desires, and resolu-
tions of the heart, of prayer of the heart, of the divine presence in
the heart, and so on. In Scripture the heart contains the fulness of
the spiritual life, which involves the whole person, with all [one's]
faculties and all [one's] activities. . . . [Moreover,] the heart . . .
remains a mystery; it is the hidden part of [the hu]man, known
only to God."[5]

With these thoughts as the backdrop of what is to come, a
few apophthegms and stories of the hidden life will be explored
in order to see what wisdom they reveal. Since there are not a lot
of stories told of hiddenness of the *ammas*, it will be necessary to
share those of the *abbas*.

STORIES AND COMMENTARY

One of the ways that one guarded the heart was to practice
the commandment of "to die to one's neighbor." "Abba Moses

[3] Matt 6:19-21 is quoted from the *New American Bible* (New York: Catholic
Book Publishing Co., 1968).

[4] Tomáš Špidlík, *The Spirituality of the Christian East: A Systematic Handbook*, Cistercian Studies 79, trans. Anthony P. Gythiel (Kalamazoo: Cistercian
Publications, 1986) 103.

[5] Ibid., 103–04, 106.

said, 'The monk must die to his neighbor and never judge him at all, in any way whatever.'"[6] "He also said, 'If the monk does not think in his heart that he is a sinner, God will not hear him.' The brother said, 'What does that mean, to think in his heart that he is a sinner?' Then the old man said, 'When someone is occupied with his own faults, he does not see those of his neighbour.'"[7]

Abba Moses was nicknamed "the Robber," for he "was a released slave who lived as a robber in Nitria; late in life he became a monk and was trained by Isidore the Priest,"[8] and was renowned for his compassion, having experienced judgment at the hands of many prior to becoming a monk. A favorite story about him concerns his attitude toward a fellow sinner:

> A brother in Scetis committed a fault. A council was called to which Abba Moses was invited, but he refused to go to it. Then the priest sent someone to say to him, "Come, for everyone is waiting for you." So he got up and went. He took a leaking jug, filled it with water and carried it with him. The others came out to meet him and said to him, "What is this, Father?" The old man said to them, "My sins run out behind me, and I do not see them, and today I am coming to judge the errors of another." When they heard that they said no more to the brother but forgave him.[9]

This story reveals how profound was the *abba's* humility or integrity of heart. He knew his past and that past, though forgiven, was not forgotten, for his remembrance of that past helped him not to sit in judgment of anyone else. Also, he is prophetic in the way that Jeremiah was, in that he acted out the teaching in such a symbolic way that none of the members of the Scetis community would forget his message about the leaking jug of water. He gave them a visual memory that was not at all hypocritical, but re-

---

[6] "Moses"—Instruction #1, *The Sayings of the Desert Fathers: The Alphabetica Collection*, Cistercian Studies 59, trans. Benedicta Ward (London & Oxford: Mowbray/U.S.A.: Cistercian Publications, 1975) 141.

[7] Ibid., "Moses"—Instruction #3, 141.

[8] Ibid., "Introduction" to "Moses," 138.

[9] Ibid., "Moses #2," 138–39.

vealed the profound truth of his life, which was known to all there anyway. Beyond that truth lay another: God is the God of forgiveness. If God were not, Moses would not have dared to live in community. His public reputation had to be forgiven by his brothers in Scetis, or else they could not accept him there. Also, Moses' self-knowledge transformed into a wisdom that he readily shared with the community. Consciousness of his own plight as sinner placed a responsibility in his life never to judge another, that is, never to "kill a neighbor" with a judgment on another's actions.

A saying similar to the teaching of Moses concerns the issue of gossip. "One of the elders said: A monk ought not to inquire how this one acts, or how that one lives. Questions like this take us away from prayer and draw us on to backbiting and chatter. There is nothing better than to keep silent."[10] Thus, exposure to the faults of others need not be expanded by gossip about those faults. Keeping silent about them when no good is done in broadcasting them is a form of hiddenness that preserves the heart's primary occupation, which is communion with God in prayer.

A reaction to this teaching is not unusual, as if one were justifying the kind of silence that fosters a conspiracy of silence about abuses in families or in the church. That is not at all what is meant in such stories. Indeed there is no advocating such silence or "keeping hidden" the secrets of such sin. Such sin needs to be exposed for what it is, no less than Moses' public life was known to the members of his community and for which he repented the rest of his life. What is at issue is not public sins of abuse and violations of human dignity kept secret, but the lesser faults of which tabloids and TV new magazines are fond—all manner of scandals that point the finger at anyone else for the sake of tickling one's ears and increasing one's sense of moral superiority. All the while, one fails to see the danger to one's own heart; preoccupation with the faults, errors, and weaknesses of others lessens the capacity of

---

[10] "Saying cxxxi," in Thomas Merton, *The Wisdom of the Desert* (Gethsemani: Abbey of Gethsemani, 1960) 74.

the heart to be focused on the one thing necessary: love of God and neighbor.

Yet another aspect of hiddenness deals with the fault of ostentation, which is well illustrated by the following story:

> Two brethren went to an elder who lived alone in Scete. And the first one said: Father, I have learned all of the Old and New Testaments by heart. The elder said to him: You have filled the air with words. The other one said: I have copied out the Old and New Testaments and have them in my cell. And to this one the elder replied: You have filled your window with parchment. But do you not know Him who said: The kingdom of God is not in words, but in power? And again, Not those who hear the Law will be justified before God but those who carry it out. They asked him, therefore, what was the way of salvation, and he said to them: The beginning of wisdom is the fear of the Lord, and humility with patience.[11]

Just picture the scene: the two brothers who come to the elder were having a competition between them about who is better, the one who has memorized the Bible, or the one who has copied it out. Notice how the elder replied to each: "you have filled the air with words . . . you have filled your window with parchment." In other words, the atmosphere around them is full of their activity—as good as each one is—rather than their being empty to receive from God. Competition is full of self-aggrandizement that serves as a substitute for awe (which is what "fear of the Lord" truly is) "and humility with patience." The combination of humility with patience is a profound one, for no one comes to humility except by the patient persevering and gradual growth in this primary virtue of hiddenness. Perhaps that is what the elder meant by "the kingdom of God is . . . in power." Just like the gospel leaven in dough, the hidden yeast expands into the whole loaf gradually and permeates the whole, but not in a way anyone can orchestrate or take credit for. Likewise, the way of salvation is the

---

[11] Ibid., "Saying cxxxiii," 74.

work of the Spirit in the realm of one's own heart or in the hearts of others. The two monks are asked to forego their competition, the measuring of holiness by their own standards; instead they are to rely on the God of the kingdom to grace their lives with the true power of living the words they have become accustomed to memorizing and writing. In that way they, too, will become as leaven in the dough of the community, participants in the power of the kingdom of God.

Still another sign of hiddenness is told in the unusual story entitled by Palladius, "The Nun Who Feigned Madness." It could have just as easily been called "The Holy Fool," for that was the nun's gift to her community. The story is related in full so one can sense its full flavor.

> 1. In this monastery [it was part of Pachomius' system of monasteries] there was another maiden who feigned madness and demon-possession. The others felt such contempt for her that they never ate with her, which pleased her entirely. Taking herself to the kitchen she used to perform every menial service and she was, as the saying goes, "the sponge of the monastery," really fulfilling the Scriptures: If any[one] among you seem to be wise in this world, let [that one] become a fool that [s/]he may be wise. She wore a rag around her head—all the others had their hair closely cropped and wore cowls. In this way she used to serve.
>
> 2. Not one of the four hundred ever saw her chewing all the years of her life. She never sat down at table or partook of a particle of bread, but she wiped up with a sponge the crumbs from the tables and was satisfied with scouring pots. She was never angry at anyone, nor did she grumble or talk, either little or much, although she was maltreated, insulted, cursed, and loathed.
>
> 3. Now an angel appeared to Saint Piteroum, the famous anchorite dwelling at Porphyrites, and said to him: "Why do you think so much of yourself for being pious and residing in a place such as this? Do you want to see someone more pious than yourself, a woman? Go to the women's monastery at Tabennisi and there you will find one with a band on her head. She is better than you are.

4. 'While being cuffed about by such a crowd she has never taken her heart off God. But you dwell here and wander about cities in your mind." And he who had never gone away left that monastery and asked the prefects to allow him to enter into the monastery of women. They admitted him, since he was well on in years and, moreover, had a great reputation.

5. So he went in and insisted upon seeing all of them. She did not appear. Finally, he said to them: "Bring them all to me, for she is missing." They told him: "We have one inside in the kitchen who is touched"—that is what they call the afflicted ones. He told them: "Bring her to me. Let me see her." They went to call her; but she did not answer, either because she knew of the incident or because it was revealed to her. They seized her forcibly and told her: "The holy Piteroum wishes to see you"—for he was renowned.

6. When she came he saw the rag on her head and, falling down at her feet, he said: "Bless me!" All the women were amazed at this and said: "Father, take no insults. She is touched." Piteroum then addressed all the women: "You are the ones who are touched! This woman is spiritual mother" [sic]—so they called them spiritually—"to both you and me and I pray that I may be deemed as worthy as she on the Day of Judgment."

7. Hearing this, they fell at his feet, confessing various things—one how she had poured the leavings of her plate over her; another had beaten her with her fists; another had blistered her nose. So they confessed various and sundry outrages. After praying for them, he left. And after a few days she was made unable to bear the praise and honor of the sisters, and all their apologizing was so burdensome to her that she left the monastery. Where she went and where she disappeared to and how she died, nobody knows.[12]

It is quite an unusual story. How is one to understand it? If one spends any time at all in a monastic community, one will discover that that community has a history of quite unusual characters,

---

[12] "#34. The Nun Who Feigned Madness," in Palladius, *The Lausiac History*, Ancient Christian Writers 34, trans. Robert T. Meyer (New York/Mahwah, N.J: Paulist Press, 1964) 96–98. www.paulistpress.com.

women who today might not have passed the MMPI assessment for entrance into the community, but who, by the grace of God, grew to be holy women. It seems that this nun was such a one. She undertakes the lowliest tasks of the community, probably tasks others were not eager to do. She is eccentric in that she wore a rag around her head and no one ever saw her chew. But, on the other hand, she put up with verbal abuse from her sisters without getting angry, grumbling, or talking back. Today, putting up with abuse without asserting oneself or speaking against it is considered neither a characteristic of holiness nor an attitude to be praised. And rightly so. However, what Palladius is pointing to as a sign of her holiness is the fact that whatever she suffered, she was not dissuaded from keeping "her heart" focused on God. Likely, many of her prayers were offered up for her community.

The key to the story is the biblical phrase from 1 Corinthians 3:18: "If anyone among you seem to be wise in this world, let that one become a fool that s/he may be wise." In the original biblical context, according to Jerome Murphy-O'Connor's commentary, the Corinthians were destroying their community by a lack of sanctity. "Sanctity is loving service, the antithesis of the divisions promoted by Corinthian wisdom speculation" based on worldly standards. Paul offers the community the folly of the cross as the standard for wisdom, based on Paul's interpretation of Job 5:13: "[God] catches the wise in their own ruses, and the designs of the crafty are routed."[13]

Neither Piteroum nor the community can assume they are the judges of holiness, for God alone sees the heart. This nun's heart remained ever centered on her God, whereas Piteroum suffered from a wandering attention and some of the nuns at the Tabennisi community were far from loving the one neighbor they despised and toward whom they did not hesitate to show their contempt.

[13] Jerome Murphy-O'Connor, "The First Letter to the Corinthians," sec. 49:24, p. 802, in *The New Jerome Biblical Commentary*, ed. Raymond E. Brown, Joseph A. Fitzmyer, and Roland E. Murphy (Englewood Cliffs, N.J.: Prentice Hall, 1990, 1968).

In the midst of Piteroum's encounter with the community, the unspoken question is, *"Who* is really touched here?" Is this nun crazy or are the attitudes manifested toward her crazy? A divine messenger revealed to Piteroum that this holy fool is none other than a "spiritual mother," an *amma*. On Judgment Day, God will reveal just who is holy and who is not. In the meantime it behooves the rest to go very lightly, if at all, on all judgments of one's own or another's holiness.

CONTEMPORARY EXAMPLE

The first time I read this story, I immediately called to mind a parallel example of holiness in my own community. When I was a novice, there was a humble oblate sister who would often be found in the old kitchen pealing potatoes. Because she was deaf and partially blind, but mostly because she suffered from intestinal cancer, she was left alone there because she smelled badly, as some of the sisters would say. One day when I was alone in the novitiate, there came a knock at the door. I opened it and found Sister Raymunda standing outside. She was as short as I was so we could see each other eye-to-eye. She motioned for me to come out into the hall. Because she was an oblate sister, she had been used to being the last in rank after the postulants and she still maintained the rules of strict cloister, thus not crossing the threshold into the novitiate.

When I came out, she looked at me and said, "Novice Mary, I was talking with Jesus, Mary, and Joseph today and asked them for a friend. They told me to come and ask you to be my friend." I was startled. I gulped and then said, "Sister Raymunda, what would a friend do for you?" She replied, "You could come and visit me sometimes." I agreed that I thought I could do that alright. Little did I know at the time what treasures those visits would hold. I learned that Raymunda was a mystic, and one unknown as that in the community at the time. When she was a young sister in the community, newly arrived from Switzerland, she discovered that there were choir nuns who found the pioneer life in rural Washington and Idaho very difficult. One day when she was at prayer, she asked the Lord to give her the share of suffering of any sister who found suffering unbearable. And in a way known only to God, God answered her prayer. I believe that one cannot ask for such a gift unless the inspiration comes from God. Two biblical images sustained Raymunda's spirituality. One was the Holy Family living the hidden life at Nazareth, which is why she often talked very personally to Jesus, Mary, and Joseph. I would often go to her door and she would be praying aloud to them, so I would wait until she finished. The other biblical image was of Jesus on the cross asking the Father to forgive those who were crucifying him, for they knew not what they were doing. In a very real way, Raymunda was my community's nun who feigned being a "holy fool," a soul not well regarded and often ignored, but whose heart was full of the suffering love of her Christ, whom she silently served and adored. Thank you, Raymunda, for the witness of your love, and thank you, all you other holy fools whoever and wherever you may be.

REFLECTION EXERCISE

I invite you to spend time with 1 Corinthians 3:10-23 on the service of God's ministers in the community. As you do so, you may wish to ask God to show you the foolishness of God's wisdom in your community, family, or congregation. Who are the hidden sources of humility, power, goodness, suffering love, and prayerfulness? Most often they do not know themselves as such; they merely serve the Lord in their quiet, unassuming manner without fanfare, sometimes with a profound awareness of their need for God and God's mercy and forgiveness. Or the Lord may take you elsewhere in your prayer time today. May that time of being together be one of ever-deepening love and recognition of how graced the relationship is, to be called into humble friendship with God.

FURTHER SCRIPTURAL PASSAGES FOR PRAYER

Romans 12:9-21   Charity in the community
2 Corinthians 11:16-33   Paul's foolishness for the Lord
2 Timothy 4:1-5 and
   Hebrews 10:30-39   On how God judges

9 Prayer and Hospitality

OPENING REFLECTION: Psalm 63:1-9

*O God of our longing, O God whom we seek, we thank you for be-
ing the God who called our foremothers in faith to found Christian
communities, a life committed to praise of you and loving care for
you in guests, pilgrims, the sick, the poor and each other. May our
own lives be reflections of this double love command—to love you
with all our hearts, souls and strength and to extend that love to our
neighbors, even as we learn to love ourselves. We trust in your grace
to sustain us in this process of ever-deepening love, as we pray in
the name who is love incarnate, Jesus Christ, our Lord. Amen.*

INTRODUCTORY REMARKS

The *ammas* manifest a twofold way of being women of wisdom: women who praise their God as their source of life, their
love, and their longing, and women who share their gifts of prayer,
self, and resources with others—a heritage to which women can
relate today. What follows is a few fragments of their prayer life
and how the fruit of their prayer was shared with others.

All the *ammas* lived lives of prayer, whether they were solitaries in the wilderness or women who started cenobitic communities in their homes or in some ascetical or monastic settlement in
or near a desert. No treatises on prayer or systematic presenta-
tions on methods of prayer have come down from them. Often in

Egypt the prayer in community consisted of regular times when the sisters gathered for *synaxes*, or periods of prayer, to pray biblical passages together, which were predominantly the Psalms.

STORIES AND COMMENTARY

For example, Jerome writes of the following regime in Paula's monasteries in Bethlehem:

> I shall now describe the order of her monastery and the method by which she turned the continence of saintly souls to her own profit. . . . Besides establishing a monastery for men, the charge of which she left to men, she divided into three companies and monasteries the numerous virgins whom she had gathered out of different provinces, some of whom are of noble birth while others belonged to the middle or lower classes. But, although they worked and had their meals separately from each other, these three companies met together for psalm-singing and prayer. After the chanting of the Alleluia—the signal by which they were summoned to the Collect—no one was permitted to remain behind. But coming either first or among the first, she used to await the arrival of the rest, urging them to diligence rather by her own modest example than by motives of fear. At dawn, at the third, sixth, and ninth hours, at evening, and at midnight they recited the Psalter each in turn. No sister was allowed to be ignorant of the psalms, and all had every day to learn a certain portion of the holy Scriptures. On the Lord's day only, they proceeded to the church beside which they lived, each company following its own mother-superior. Returning home in the same order, they then devoted themselves to their allotted tasks, and made garments either for themselves or else for others.[1]

The memorization of Scriptures was common in the whole of the early tradition. Part of the reason for this was practical, given that

---

[1] "Paula the Elder: An Ascetic Pilgrim to Rome and Bethlehem," in *Handmaids of the Lord: Contemporary Descriptions of Feminine Asceticism in the First Six Christian Centuries*, Cistercian Studies 143, trans. and ed. Joan M. Petersen (Kalamazoo: Cistercian Publications, 1996) 147.

making books out of parchment was a long and slow process of production that included scraping the skins, drying them, making dyes for ink, plucking and cutting quills, ruling the parchment, and, finally, the actual calligraphy. Consequently, the scrolls themselves were few in number and very valuable. If members knew the Psalms by heart, then fewer needed the large, unwieldy manuscript books from which to recite. The other reason was that when one memorized the biblical passages, then one always had a reservoir of the living Word upon which to draw for *lectio* as one engaged in other activities of monastic living. These activities included carding, spinning, and weaving wool, cotton, and linen into cloth, and plaiting reeds from which to make rope and baskets.

In the above passage, Paula resorted to three different houses of nuns based on their rank in society. It was likely that the noble ladies devoted more of their time to copying the Bible and biblical commentaries, while their servants, who were never allowed to wait on their own mistresses, were engaged in manual labor. Despite this kind of separation for their work and for the meals, all were together in the main engagement of their monastic life, that of the singing of the praises of God.

Besides what would later come to be called the Divine Office, by which monastic men and women kept the rule of faith—"to pray always" (1 Thess 5:17)—there were the vigils, that is, the times of intense keeping watch in prayer with the Lord before major feast days and through Saturday night, in anticipation of the great day of Resurrection each week—Sunday.

For example, Melania the Younger, in the monastery of women she established at the Mount of Olives, where her grandmother had had a monastery,

> used to exhort the sisters to be especially eager on Sundays and the other great feast days to employ themselves in the earnest singing of the psalms, saying, "If it is good not to be negligent in the daily office, we ought with even more reason to sing the psalms a little more on Sundays and on the other feast days than in our normal office."

By speaking this way, she so encouraged them in their enthusiasm by her sound teaching that if ever the blessed lady wished to spare them their vigils on account of their great weariness, they themselves would not agree to it, saying, "Just as you continually consider our bodily needs day after day, so much the more should we not let anything drop out of our daily office, where spiritual matters are concerned." The blessed lady rejoiced greatly when she saw their generous decision in the Lord.[2]

Gerontius, monastic author of the *Life of Melania the Younger*, idealized Melania and her leadership, often skipping over problematic issues in the community or Melania's need to oversee every aspect of the ascetical life, even though she had delegated responsibility of the community to others.[3]

Besides the times of chanting the psalms and the keeping of vigils, several stories of *ammas* speak to the practice of private prayer. Amma Theodora speaks of the struggle to grow in the practice of prayer that eventually leads to peace, or what was called *apatheia*, the freedom from besetting temptations that lead to discouragement in the pursuit of seeking God in all things.

She . . . said, "It is good to live in peace, for the wise [person] practises perpetual prayer. It is truly a great thing for a virgin or a monk to live in peace, especially for the younger ones. However, you should realize that as soon as you intend to live in peace, at once evil comes and weighs down your soul through *accidie*, faintheartedness, and evil thoughts. It also attacks your body through sickness, debility, weakening of the knees, and all the members. It dissipates the strength of soul and body, so that one believes one is

---

[2] "The Life of the Holy Melania by Gerontius," in *Handmaids of the Lord*, 340.

[3] A case in point is when Melania appointed a superior of monastery, but "When the Superior was a little too strict, Melania vigorously devoted herself to supplying their bodily needs. She took such care of the more delicate sisters that she hid whatever they needed and carefully put it in each one's cell, under the straw on the floor. When they cam [sic] in, they found everything she had prepared for their comfort, without their Mother knowing about it." See *Handmaids of the Lord*, 336.

ill and no longer able to pray. But if we are vigilant, all these temptations fall away. There was, in fact a monk who was seized by cold and fever every time he began to pray, and he suffered from headaches, too. In this condition, he said to himself, 'I am ill, and near to death; so now I will get up before I die and pray.' By reasoning in this way, he did violence to himself and prayed. When he had finished, the fever abated also. So by reasoning in this way, the brother resisted, and prayed and was able to conquer his thoughts."[4]

It takes a lifetime to grow into an attitude of serenity in the midst of temptation in which the diminishments of aging are not a cause of complaint, but an ever-growing awareness that the time of God's calling one home is near. No matter what age one is, one is subject to temptation; one always stands in need of God's mercy, salvation, and grace in order to be vigilant and to continue to keep praying, even when one does not feel like it.

As Laura Swan states in her book, *The Forgotten Desert Mothers,*

> Prayer was a continuous way of life in the desert. It was intentionally cultivated until it became second nature. Prayer involved the hard work of learning a new language—the language of heaven. For the ascetic, prayer was not merely the speaking of words. It was the heart yearning for God, reaching out in hopeful openness to being touched by God. Prayer was for the Holy Spirit breathing through the inner spirit of the ascetic and returning to God with yearnings of intimacy.

> The ascetic sought to cultivate a silent, passionate, and burning love for God experienced in deep and nurturing solitude. The atmosphere for rich prayer was a simple quiet voice, not a noisy inner crowd. Physical as well as inner stillness and quiet were necessary. The words of prayer were brief and straight from the heart. Praying the psalms, intercession, contemplation, and silent awareness

---

[4] "Theodora #3," in *The Sayings of the Desert Fathers: The Alphabetical Collection,* Cistercian Studies 59, trans. Benedicta Ward (London & Oxford: Mowbray/ U.S.A.: Cistercian Publications, 1975) 85.

of God's presence were all expressions of prayer in the desert and monastery.[5]

As these women grew in "silent awareness of God's presence," they also grew in hospitality of heart which, in turn, enabled them to receive others as gifts of God.

Besides prayer, no other practice of early monasticism was as essential as hospitality, as Cassian has taught.

> Abba Cassian related the following: "The holy Germanus and I went to Egypt, to visit an old man. Because he offered us hospitality we asked him, 'Why do you not keep the rule of fasting, when you receive visiting brothers, as we have received it in Palestine?' He replied, 'Fasting is always to hand but you I cannot have with me always. Furthermore, fasting is certainly a useful and necessary thing, but it depends on our choice while the law of God lays it upon us to do the works of charity. Thus receiving Christ in you, I ought to serve you [with] all diligence, but when I have taken leave of you, I can resume the rule of fasting again. For "Can the wedding guests fast while the bridegroom is with them, but when the bridegroom is taken from them, then they will fast in that day"'" (Mark 2:19-20).[6]

Cassian clearly teaches that one entertains Christ every time one makes time in one's schedule; one's task or occupation is to host the stranger, guest, or poor person, who appears most often unexpectedly in our midst. In ancient Christianity, one was expected to attend to this living embodiment of Christ before oneself. Thereby one lived the Lord's directive: "Whatsoever you did for one of my least ones, you have done to me" (Matt 25:40). Christians for centuries have heard the call to care for the least ones as the criterion for reward at the Last Judgment, and consequently have been given a vital reason for keeping vigilant for the coming of the Lord in the other.

---

[5] Laura Swan, *The Forgotten Desert Mothers: Sayings, Lives, and Stories of Early Christian Women* (New York/Mahwah, N.J.: Paulist Press, 2001) 27–28. www.paulistpress.com.

[6] "Cassian #1," in *The Sayings of the Desert Fathers*, 113.

A delightful story of the bestowal of a gift from the grace of prayer is told of Macrina by a soldier to Gregory of Nyssa as they were returning from Macrina's funeral. The soldier stated that one day he and his wife went to visit the monasteries established by Macrina, along with their little daughter,

> who was having trouble with her eye as the result of an infectious illness. She was a hideous and pitiful sight, because the cornea of her eye had become swollen round the pupil and had taken on a livid hue as the result of the disease. Once we had entered this holy dwelling, we were separated—my wife and I—according to sex, for our visits to the people who were leading the life of philosophy there. I was in the men's quarters, of which your brother Peter was in charge, while my wife went into the virgins' house and met the saint there. After a certain interval, we decided that it was time to leave this place of retreat, and we were already on the point of departing when a proof of friendship came to us from both sides. Your brother told me to stay and to share the meal of the philosophers, and the holy woman would not let my wife go, but taking my little girl on her lap, refused to let them leave before she had set a meal before them and offered them the riches of philosophy. As was natural, she caressed the child; as she put her lips to her eyes, she noticed that the pupils were diseased. "If you grant us the favor of sharing our common table," she said, "I will give you a reward . . . a remedy . . . which is powerful for healing eye-diseases."[7]

Of course, with a little persuasion the couple stayed for the meal and then bid their host and hostess respectively farewell. When husband and wife were together walking back to their home and the wife was relating all that happened,

> she cut short her account, saying, "What have we done? How could we forget the promise which has been given us, the promise of a lotion as a remedy?" I was most distressed at our carelessness and was ordering one of our servants to run back quickly for the

[7] "A Letter from Gregory, Bishop of Nyssa on the Life of Saint Macrina," in *Handmaids of the Lord*, 80–81.

remedy, when the child, who was in her nurse's arms, happened to look at her mother, who fixed her eyes on the child. "Stop worrying over your carelessness," she said in a loud voice, filled with both joy and surprise, "Look, we lack nothing that has been promised us. The true remedy for healing her illness is treatment by prayer; that she has been given, and it has already had its effect. No trace of the eye-trouble is left, as the eye has been made clean by the saint's remedy." . . . I recalled the unbelievable miracles in the Gospels and said, "What is there surprising about sight being given to the blind through the hand of God, when his handmaid brings about these healings by her own faith and achieves something which is only a little less than these miracles?"[8]

Macrina's gift, brought about by her prayer and healing kiss of the child's eye, was given in exchange for the opportunity to offer hospitality to this holy family, if you will. Because the couple were received as Christ by the *amma* and her brother, the couple, in turn, experienced the healing of Christ in the person of the *amma*. Only one who had prayed all her life to serve Christ would recognize Christ's visitation to her as guest. Thus her prayer bore fruit in the giving of sight to the little girl, who otherwise would have suffered blindness.

The last story has to do with a "God-fearing woman" whose discernment and strength of character saved a monk's vocation while she healed his disease.

> Someone said, "[A monk] was once bitten by a snake, and went to a certain city to be cured. He was received by a pious and God-fearing woman, and she healed him. When the pain had subsided a bit, the devil began to suggest things to him, and he wanted to touch the woman's hand. She said to him, 'Do not do this, father; have regard for Christ. Think of the grief and contrition you will experience when you are in your cell. Think of the groans and tears which will be yours.' When he heard these and similar things from her, the attack left him and he was greatly embarrassed, wanting to flee because he could not look her in the eye. She, with the mercy

[8] Ibid., 81–82.

of Christ, said to him, 'Do not be ashamed that you still have progress to make. Those things did not come from your own pure soul,
but the suggestion was made through the devil's wickedness.' Thus
she healed him without scandal and sent him on his way with provisions for the journey" (John Moschus, *Pratum Spirituale*, 204
[PG 87, 3:3093–095]).[9]

There are quite a few stories in the *Desert Fathers* that warn
monks against being in the presence of women, primarily because the young disciples, newly come to the desert, still had not
grown sufficiently in interiority so as to not have sexual fantasies
about women, let alone conduct themselves appropriately in the
presence of a woman. So the story just related is refreshing from
the point of view of a woman who becomes the instrument of a
monk's retaining his vocation. How did she know that the suggestion to touch her was from the tempter? She had to be a discerning
woman of prayer, graced with insight. Note her first words, "Do
not do this, father; have regard for Christ." Christ is to be the focus of their relationship, she as healer to his physical illness. Also,
there is that loving awareness after her words brought on by the
monk's embarrassment over his behavior: "she, with the mercy of
Christ," spoke to him. She could distinguish the source of the possible temptation from the person, who was a good-souled monk.
Finally, at the end, she extends to him hospitality of provisions
after the hospitality of her heart had not only cured his illness,
but also his temptation. She offered him the intimacy of loving
acceptance that overrode his intention for sexual intimacy. The
narrator closes this encounter with the words, "Thus she healed
him without scandal and sent him on his way with provisions for
the journey." She has been for the monk the Christ who healed
him of the snake bite, the Christ who did not condemn him for his
temptation, and the Christ who fed him and sent him on his way.
She has served as *amma*, midwife to his whole being.

---

[9] Cited by Columba Stewart, "The Portrayal of Women in the Sayings and Stories of the Desert," *Vox Benedictina* 2.1 (January 1985) 16–17.

CONTEMPORARY EXAMPLE

Several years ago, while enrolled in a course entitled, "The Biblical Bases of Peace and Justice," I found myself sitting next to Maria. Over lunch one day, we began exploring our insights from the class. I discovered that Maria had been raised by communist parents, first in Hungary and then in the former Yugoslavia; she discovered that I was a Benedictine sister. My early Catholic training had deeply ingrained in me the need to pray for the conversion of communists and to view them all as atheists. Yet over the course of several more lunches, my prejudices were dramatically overturned. Conversation about Maria's recent battle with cancer surfaced in her daily morning ritual of quiet time. She began to share that she listened for a voice deep within her that brought her peace and guidance. The more Maria shared, the more I realized that I was in the presence of a deeply contemplative woman who, even without formal religious training in a spiritual tradition, had been visited by the Divine in her prayer. I was able to present her with a possible language for her experience from my monastic tradition. Our mutual receptivity to each other's culture, experience, and background allowed for an enriching exchange of gifts between us. One day she said that I was one of the few sisters she had met; the others belonged to an order that was establishing a hospice in the town in which she lived before immigrating to Canada. Maria acted as a go-between with the communist officials in the town on behalf of these sisters. After telling me the story, I discovered that one of the sisters for whom Maria was negotiating was none other than Mother Theresa of Calcutta!

REFLECTION EXERCISES

I invite you to reflect on an occasion in which you grew in the realization of Christ's presence in others in a new or deeper way. How did that occasion come about? What situation, ministry, or chance encounter brought you face-to-face with the grace to offer hospitality? What happened to you as a result of this occasion? How were you able to see a stranger, guest, pilgrim, or poor person in a whole new light? How was this person contributing to you? If you are so moved, you may want to write a prayer of thanksgiving for Christ's visitation of you through this person.

Or you may wish to recall an occasion when you experienced a deeper call to prayer, either because of a circumstance or because God spoke to you in a retreat, a reading, or conversation. Where then did the Spirit lead you? How did your prayer change? What did you learn about God's presence with you, in you, through you? As you reflect upon this occasion, ask yourself what the fruit of your prayer relationship with the Divine One has been? If you are moved to do so, you may want to write a prayer of thanksgiving for God's loving nudge to grow closer to the Divine One.

FURTHER SCRIPTURAL PASSAGES FOR PRAYER

Psalms 42 and 84   Longing for God

Hospitality:
Genesis 18:1-15   The visitation at Mamre
Hebrews 13:1-3   Final commendations
Luke 19:1-10   Jesus' invitation to Zacchaeus
Matthew 25:31-46   The Last Judgment scene

Conclusion—The Visitation

OPENING REFLECTION: Luke 1:39-45, 56a

O God of our foremothers in faith, Elizabeth and Mary, thank you for gifting us with their shared joy in bearing new life within them: one, the forerunner proclaiming a message of repentance, the other, the source of our salvation. Elizabeth and Mary, we thank you for your full-hearted "yes" to life, one in your old age, the other in your youth. Such a surprise God had in store for you two, yet you kept these things in your hearts, waiting for the day when you could share them in the blessedness of your conversations together. May the God of your faith, bless us with new life, in whatever forms that may come to us and may we, like you, say a full-hearted "yes." We ask this through your intercession, trusting in the name of the One who makes hope possible, Jesus Christ, our Lord. Amen.

REMARKS

In this meeting of two great spiritual mothers, one ponders the mystery of significant salvific moments in one's faith journey. You have been remembering the salvation moments in your life with the Lord, who saves. In every chapter you have been invited to ponder the mystery of a significant relationship in your faith that has called you to an awareness of God's tender, cherishing care of you. It has been good to ponder these sacred moments.

After a time of intense prayer or retreat, one moves into another aspect of one's life as one returns to the dailiness of loving and caring for one's home and its many guests and needs, or to one's ministry among God's people, with attentiveness to the needs there. I have noticed how often, after a time of retreat, I find myself a bit irritable or discombobulated, longing for the quiet of retreat days. It is as if that intensity of silence has pulled me deep into the pool of prayer, and I am reluctant to be called back to attending to God's holy ones. But Jesus sends us down the mountain of transfiguration, where conversation with Moses and Elijah was so sweet, just as he did the disciples to await him so that we might await those around us.

For some moments, before descending the mountain, let yourself attend to the presence of Mary and Elizabeth. In every community, family, or parish, there are the younger women and ones new to the faith journey who, like Mary, have set out in haste to the "the hill country" (Luke 1:39)[1] of your monastery, congregation, or place of service and have entered eager to greet you. The older women, perhaps in age or in length of commitment, like Elizabeth, hear the sounds of the new ones' joy, new life, and hopes for the days ahead, and the *ammas* are moved with stirrings of joy. Those who thought their life was barren and could not conceive of new life being possible in old age become surprised by God's gift to bring new life to old bones, old dreams, and age-old traditions.

In the exchange of hospitality between newcomers—old and young alike—and those who have lived most of their lives in this way of life, each "proclaims the greatness of the Lord" (Luke 1:46). Each experiences God looking upon her lowliness and prays, "God who is mighty has done great things for me; holy is God's name" (Luke 1:49).

Spending time pondering the deeds of the Lord is sheer grace that brings a renewed showering of God's love. I hope that by praying with the stories of the *ammas* you have come to proclaim the great deeds of God in your own life—how God has sustained you in prayer, has spoken to you in precious, remembered words

---

[1] *New American Bible* (New York: Catholic Book Publishing Co., 1968). All quotations from Scripture in this chapter are from this edition.

from Scripture, and called you to a deeper awareness of how God is in the midst of the community whenever it gathers and remembers.

Whenever you hear beautiful singing, either of the Divine Office or a congregation at worship, know that harmonious praying together witnesses that "God's name is holy" (Luke 1:49). The lovely stories of the *ammas*, which you have savored, are a reminder of the great love to which all are called. The care of your home—beautifying it with flower gardens, touches of color, and artwork—can bring a sense of at-homeness that is inviting to strangers and guests alike.

Friendship, that wonderful gift exchanged between young and old, invites conversations around the things that really matter and presages the very visitation of God. Asking for prayer and support invites another to contribute to your own sense of God's nearness.

You have heard stories of the beautiful deaths of some of the wise ones who have gone home to God. They echo in their dying Macrina's last prayer: "It is You, O Lord, who have freed us from the fear of death. You have made our life here the beginning of our true life. You grant our bodies to rest in sleep for a season and you rouse our bodies *again at the last trumpet.*"[2]

You have been blessed to see God's graciousness in your life. May your gratitude move you to share your own wisdom with the receptive hearts around you. May whoever comes to your door seeking nourishment for both body and soul find a waiting elder, eager to give out of abundance. It is clear to me that we extend God's loving heart and hands to those with whom we work, play, and live.

I hope that you have someone to hear the stories of your own *ammas*, those elders of wisdom, courage, and prayerful honesty, who have called you to be more than you ever thought you could

---

[2] "A Letter from Gregory, Bishop of Nyssa on the Life of Saint Macrina," in *Handmaids of the Lord: Contemporary Descriptions of Feminine Asceticism in the First Six Centuries*, Cistercian Studies 143, trans. and ed. Joan M. Petersen (Kalamazoo: Cistercian Publications, 1996) 70.

be. Thank you for the gift to be able to share my *ammas* with you, both those wise "midwives" of the desert, but also the dear ones of my own community and life experience.

"Blessed are you among women and blessed is the fruit" (Luke 1:42) of your life-giving midwifing of others in faith. May God continue to send you the folks hungry for the living words of the Gospel: the poor and lowly to whom you minister in your social justice ministries; the men and women of all ages whom you teach in your church work; and the wide-eyed children, both far and near, who love to sit in your presence and bask for a few moments in the tangible holiness that is your gift to them, whether you are always aware of it or not.

Whether young, old, or in the middle, may the Lord ever uphold you as Israel, the Lord's servant. May you continue to remain faithful to your family, community, and congregation until God calls you to return home, where there will be only eternal welcomes and no goodbyes. May you always be blessed with *ammas* who enkindle your faith, remind you of how beloved you are in God's eyes, as well as their own, and who gently, yet courageously, recall you to be God's gift of prayerful and welcoming hospitality that you are. And may each one grow into the wisdom and holiness of our early foremother, Mary, "who trusted that the Lord's words to her would be fulfilled . . . " (Luke 1:45).

In the Jewish tradition, blessings were a natural part of women greeting each other. Certainly, Mary and Elizabeth blessed each other on first meeting and then again when they bid each other farewell and, most likely, many times in between. I invite you to find someone today and bless him/her with a sign of the cross on the forehead; then let him/her do likewise to you. I invite you to call on God to bless your sister/brother in Christ in whatever words come to you as the grace you wish her/him to receive and then let her/him bless you.

Should you be interested in further reading on the desert *ammas*, there is a list of books and articles in the bibliography at the back of this book.

Bibliography on the Desert *Ammas*

I. PRIMARY SOURCES IN TRANSLATION

Egeria: Diary of a Pilgrimage. Ancient Christian Writers 38. Trans. George E. Gingras. New York: Newman Press, 1970. www.paulistpresscom.

Egeria's Travels. Trans. John Wilkinson. London: SPCK, 1971.

____. "The Pilgrimage of Egeria." In *A Lost Tradition: Women Writers of the Early Church*. Trans. and ed. Patricia Wilson-Kastner. Lanham, Md.: University Press of America, 1981.

Gerontius. *The Life of Melania the Younger*. Studies in Women and Religion 14. Trans. Elizabeth A. Clark. N.Y.: The Edwin Mellen Press, 1984.

____. "The Life of Holy Melania by Gerontius," 311–58. In *Handmaids of the Lord: Holy Women in Late Antiquity & the Early Middle Ages*. 311–58. Cistercian Studies 143. Trans. Joan M. Petersen. Kalamazoo: Cistercian Publications, 1996.

Gregory, Bishop of Nyssa. *The Life of Saint Macrina*. Trans. Kevin Corrigan. Toronto: Peregrina Publishing Co., 1987.

____. "A Letter from Gregory, Bishop of Nyssa on the Life of Saint Macrina." In *Handmaids of the Lord*.

Jerome. St. Jerome: Letters and Select Works. Nicene and Post-Nicene Fathers 2.6. Trans. W. H. Fremantle. Edinburgh: T & T Clark/Grand Rapids, Mich.: Wm. B. Eerdmans Publishing Co., 1989 reprint.

Jerome. *"Ancillae Domini* in the Roman Empire: Letters of Saint Jerome to Ascetic Women in the Roman Empire," 87–281. In *Handmaids of the Lord*.

Lives of the Desert Fathers: Historia Monachorum in Aegypto. Cistercian Studies 34. Trans. Norman Russell. London & Oxford: Mowbray/ U.S.A.: Cistercian Publications, 1980.

Palladius: The Lausiac History. Ancient Christian Writers 34. Trans. Robert T. Meyer. New York/Mahwah, N.J.: Paulist Press, 1964. www.paulistpress.com.

Pseudo-Athanasius. *The Life of The Blessed & Holy Syncletica.* Part One: The Translation. Trans. Elizabeth Bryson Bongie. Toronto: Peregrina Publishing Co., 1996, 1998 second edition. Part Two: A Study of the Life. By Mary Schaffer. Toronto: Peregrina Publishing Co., 2001.

The Sayings of the Desert Fathers: The Alphabetical Collection. Cistercian Studies 59. Trans. Benedicta Ward. Kalamazoo: Cistercian Publications, 1975.

The Wisdom of the Desert Fathers: Systematic Sayings from the Anonymous Series of the Apophthegmata Patrum. Trans. Benedicta Ward. Fairacres & Oxford: SLG Press, 1975.

The Wisdom of the Desert: Sayings from the Desert Fathers of the Fourth Century. Trans. Thomas Merton. Gethsemani: The Abbey of Gethsemani, 1960.

Ward, Benedicta. *Harlots of the Desert: A Study of Repentance in Early Monastic Sources.* London & Oxford: Mowbray, 1987.

II. SECONDARY READINGS ABOUT DESERT *AMMAS*

Brown, Peter. *The Body and Society: Men, Women and Sexual Renunciation in Early Christianity.* Lectures on the History of Religions, N.S. 13. New York: Columbia University Press, 1988.

Clark, Elizabeth A. *Ascetic Piety and Women's Faith: Essays on Late Ancient Christianity.* Studies in Women and Religion 20. Lewiston, N.Y.: The Edwin Mellen Press, 1986.

Cloke, Gillian. *This Female Man of God: Women and Spiritual Power in the Patristic Age, AD 350–450.* London/New York: Routledge, 1995.

Coon, Lynda L. *Sacred Fictions: Holy Women and Hagiography in Late Antiquity,* Philadelphia: University of Pennsylvania Press, 1997.

Corrigan, Kevin. "Saint Macrina: The Hidden Face Behind the Tradition." *Vox Benedictina* 5.1 (January 1988) 12–28.

Elliott, Alison Goddard. *Roads to Paradise: Reading the Lives of the Early Saints.* Hanover & London: Published for Brown University Press by University Press of New England, 1987.

Elm, Susanna. 'Virgins of God': The Making of Asceticism in Late Antiquity. Oxford Classical Monographs. Oxford: Clarendon Press, 1994.

Forman, Mary. "Amma Syncletica: A Spirituality of Experience." Vox Benedictina 10.2 (Winter 1993) 199–237. Also, reprinted, 259–82. In On Pilgrimage: The Best of Ten Years of Vox Benedictina 1984–1993. Ed. Margot King. Toronto: Peregrina Publications, 1994.

_____. "Purity of Heart in the Life and Words of Amma Syncletica." In Purity of Heart in Early Ascetic and Monastic Literature. Ed. Harriet A. Luckman and Linda Kulzer, 161–74. Collegeville: Liturgical Press, 1999.

Gould, Graham. "Women in the Writings of the Fathers: Language, Belief and Reality." In Women in the Church. Ed. W. J. Sheils and Diana Wood, 1–13. Oxford: Basil Blackwell, 1990.

Kelly, J.N.D. Jerome: His Life, Writings and Controversies. New York/San Francisco: Harper & Row, 1975.

Murphy, Francis X. "Melania the Elder, a biographical note." Traditio 5 (1947) 59–78.

Rader, Rosemary. Breaking Boundaries: Male/Female Friendship in Early Christian Communities. Theological Inquiries: Studies in Contemporary Biblical and Theological Problems. Ed. Lawrence Boadt. New York/Ramsey, N.J./Toronto: Paulist Press, 1983. www.paulistpress.com.

Saint-Laurent, George E. "The Pilgrimage of Egeria." In Word and Spirit: A Monastic Review 6—Monasticism: A Historical Overview. 24–40. Still River, Mass.: St. Bede's Publications, 1984.

Simpson, Jane. "Women and Asceticism in the Fourth Century: A Question of Interpretation." The Journal of Religious History 15.1 (June 1988) 38–60.

Soler, Josep M. "The desert mothers and spiritual maternity." Theology Digest 36.1 (Spring 1989) 31–35.

Stewart, Columba. "The Portrayal of Women in the Sayings and Stories of the Desert." Vox Benedictina 2.1 (January 1985) 5–23.

Swan, Laura. The Forgotten Desert Mothers: Sayings, Lives, and Stories of Early Christian Women. New York/Mahwah, N.J.: Paulist Press, 2001.